Studying Student Attrition

Ernest T. Pascarella, *Editor*

NEW DIRECTIONS FOR INSTITUTIONAL RESEARCH
Sponsored by the Association for Institutional Research
MARVIN W. PETERSON, *Editor-in-Chief*

Number 36, December 1982

Paperback sourcebooks in
The Jossey-Bass Higher Education Series

Jossey-Bass Inc., Publishers
San Francisco • Washington • London

Studying Student Attrition
Volume IX, Number 4, December 1982
    Ernest T. Pascarella, *Editor*

New Directions for Institutional Research Series
Marvin W. Peterson, *Editor-in-Chief*

New Directions for Institutional Research (publication number
USPS 098-830) is published quarterly by Jossey-Bass Inc.,
Publishers, and is sponsored by the Association for Institutional
Research. The volume and issue numbers above are included for
the convenience of libraries. Second-class postage rates paid at
San Francisco, California, and at additional mailing offices.

Correspondence:
Subscriptions, single-issue orders, change of address notices,
undelivered copies, and other correspondence should be sent to
New Directions Subscriptions, Jossey-Bass Inc., Publishers,
433 California Street, San Francisco, California 94104.

Editorial correspondence should be sent to the Editor-in-Chief,
Marvin W. Peterson, Center for the Study of Higher Education,
University of Michigan, Ann Arbor, Michigan 48109.

Library of Congress Catalogue Card Number LC 81-48576
International Standard Serial Number ISSN 0271-0579
International Standard Book Number ISBN 87589-906-4

Cover art by Willi Baum
Manufactured in the United States of America

Ordering Information

The paperback sourcebooks listed below are published quarterly and can be ordered either by subscription or as single copies.

Subscriptions cost $35.00 per year for institutions, agencies, and libraries. Individuals can subscribe at the special rate of $21.00 per year *if payment is by personal check.* (Note that the full rate of $35.00 applies if payment is by institutional check, even if the subscription is designated for an individual.) Standing orders are accepted.

Single copies are available at $7.95 when payment accompanies order, and *all single-copy orders under $25.00 must include payment.* (California, Washington, D.C., New Jersey, and New York residents please include appropriate sales tax.) For billed orders, cost per copy is $7.95 plus postage and handling. (Prices subject to change without notice.)

To ensure correct and prompt delivery, all orders must give either the *name of an individual* or an *official purchase order number.* Please submit your order as follows:

Subscriptions: specify series and subscription year.
Single Copies: specify sourcebook code and issue number (such as, IR8).

Mail orders for United States and Possessions, Latin America, Canada, Japan, Australia, and New Zealand to:
    Jossey-Bass Inc., Publishers
    433 California Street
    San Francisco, California 94104

Mail orders for all other parts of the world to:
    Jossey-Bass Limited
    28 Banner Street
    London EC1Y 8QE

New Directions for Institutional Research Series
Marvin W. Peterson, *Editor-in-Chief*

Contents

Editor's Notes

Given the magnitude and economic consequences of the dropout phenomenon, it is not surprising that substantial research and theoretical writing have focused on student attrition from postsecondary institutions. In the past decade, a number of reviews have been written (for example, Cope and Hannah, 1975; Lenning, Beal, and Sauer, 1980; Ramist, 1981; Tinto, 1975) that provide excellent syntheses of a large and growing body of research findings. By synthesizing the correlates of persistence/withdrawal behavior and suggesting fruitful directions for further research, such reviews clearly make important contributions to institutional research. At the same time, however, the existing literature has only rarely given sufficient attention to the issues involved in actually studying student persistence/withdrawal behavior at the institutional level.

For the institutional researcher studying student attrition, it is seldom enough to know merely what the existing research literature says in a general sense. He or she is confronted with a plethora of specific issues that must be dealt with (for example, adequate operational definitions of withdrawal versus persistence, theoretical considerations, selecting and measuring variables, and designing and carrying out data collections and data analyses). It is one thing to be familiar with the generalizations that can be drawn from college attrition research; it is quite another to translate these general trends into investigations that shed light on the persistence/withdrawal process in specific institutional settings.

The purpose of this volume of *New Directions for Institutional Research* is to address some of the central theoretical, methodological, and data-analytic concerns involved in studying student attrition, and to give institutional researchers and others involved in studying student persistence/withdrawal behavior a series of theoretical approaches, considerations for variable selection and measurement, research designs, and data-analytic tools useful for studying student withdrawal at the institutional level.

In the first chapter, Vincent Tinto outlines and discusses the many different perspectives from which the dropout phenomenon can be defined. The individual student's withdrawal from an institution (or from postsecondary education generally) may have a number of different implications both for the student and for the institution, and not all these implications are harmful. Thus institutional researchers must give considerable thought to what they define as dropout behaviors.

In the second chapter, John Bean presents and discusses a number of recent theoretical models of the dropout process. Such models can be particularly useful to institutional researchers and others studying the attrition phenomenon, in that the models provide a parsimonious guide to the selection of variables and to their relationships in student persistence/withdrawal behavior.

The problems and issues of variable selection and measurement are considered in the following chapter, by Oscar Lenning. He lists and discusses a wide range of potentially important predictor variables. He also suggests considerations that need to be taken into account in selecting variables and addresses practical measurement concerns related to reliability, validity, and multiple measurement of constructs.

Patrick Terenzini's chapter deals with the design of attrition studies and appropriate data-analytic procedures. He presents practical as well as conceptual advantages and liabilities of "autopsy" and of cross-sectional and longitudinal designs in attrition research, as well as uses of multivariate statistical procedures for analyzing the data yielded from attrition studies. He includes such procedures as multiple regression, discriminant analysis, and path analysis.

Philip Beal and Ernest Pascarella offer a chapter that discusses the effectiveness of some institutional interventions designed to increase persistence. They also present a practical procedure for verifying and determining the effectiveness of such institutional interventions.

Finally, David W. Chapman presents a comprehensive list of references for researchers who are studying student attrition.

Ernest T. Pascarella
Editor

References

Cope, R., and Hannah, W. *Revolving College Doors: The Causes and Consequences of Dropping Out, Stopping Out, and Transferring.* New York: Wiley, 1975.

Lenning, O., Beal, P., and Sauer, K. *Retention and Attrition: Evidence for Action and Research.* Boulder, Colo.: National Center for Higher Education Management Systems, 1980.

Ramist, L. *College Student Attrition and Retention.* College Board Report No. 81-1. New York: College Entrance Examination Board, 1981.

Tinto, V. "Dropouts from Higher Education: A Theoretical Synthesis of Recent Research. *Review of Educational Research,* 1975, *45,* 89–125.

Ernest T. Pascarella is professor of evaluation research,
College of Education, University of Illinois–Chicago.

There is a great variety of behaviors designated by the label "dropout,"
but not all these leaving behaviors should be defined this way, nor do
they all deserve institutional action.

Defining Dropout:
A Matter of Perspective

Vincent Tinto

The field of dropout research is in a state of disarray, in large measure because we have been unable to agree about what behaviors constitute an appropriate definition of dropout. The result has been confusion and contradiction as to the character and causes of dropout from higher education. For example, while some studies have claimed that the likelihood of dropping out is inversely related to ability, others have argued that the reverse is true — namely, that the brightest students are most likely to drop out from college. Although it is obvious that both conclusions cannot be true for the same set of behaviors, it took some time for researchers to discover that these studies were in fact describing two very different types of behavior, that is, academic dismissal and voluntary withdrawal. As in other situations, researchers concerned with attrition have frequently applied the term "dropout" to quite distinct forms of leaving behavior.

What follows here is an attempt to bring some order to the question of what constitutes dropout. We will ask not only how dropout may be defined, but also how that definition may vary among different interested parties con-

The author is indebted to a number of individuals whose comments on earlier drafts of the manuscript proved invaluable in subsequent revisions, particularly to Gerald Grant, Thomas Green, Ernest Pascarella, Nick Smith, and Patrick Terenzini.

E. Pascarella (Ed.). *New Directions for Institutional Research: Studying Student Attrition,* no. 36.
San Francisco: Jossey-Bass, December 1982.

cerned with the character of dropout from higher education. For the purposes of the present discussion, those parties will be taken to be the individuals who exhibit leaving behaviors, the institutional officials concerned with the reduction of attrition from their campuses, and state and national officials charged with the establishment of policies designed to reduce attrition at a regional or national level.

Dropout as Individual Behavior

The starting point in developing a definition of dropout appropriate to the perspective of the individual is the recognition that the meanings a student attributes to his or her behavior may differ substantially from those that an external observer attaches to the same behavior. The simple act of leaving an institution may have multiple and quite disparate meanings to those who are involved in or are affected by that behavior. Although an observer such as an institutional official may define a leaving behavior as a failure to complete a given course of study, students may understand leaving as a positive step toward goal completion; their understanding of a given leaving behavior differs because their goals and interests differ.

Dropout and the Character of Individual Goals

The definition of dropout from the individual perspective must make reference to the goals and intentions with which individuals enter the higher educational system. A great diversity of goals characterizes the intentions of entering students. Some goals are neither coterminus with degree completion nor necessarily compatible with those of the institution into which first entry is made. Moreover, goals may not be perfectly clear to the person entering college, and they may change during the college years.

Within any institution, there will always be some individuals whose educational goals are either more limited or more extensive than those of the institution into which first entry is gained. Among students with more limited educational goals, participation in higher education often involves accumulating a limited number of credits for occupational certification and/or job promotion. For part-time working students, participation may require the acquisition of a specific (rather than a general) set of skills needed for on-the-job activities. For these students, as for others, completing a degree program may not be a desired end; short-term rather than full-term attendance may be sufficient to achieve their goals. The same situation may apply to those individuals whose educational goals exceed those of the institution. Within the two-year college sector, in particular, large numbers of students may enter institutions with the intention of transferring to other colleges. In either case, it is not surprising that many of these students leave before completing degrees. They have accomplished what they came to the institution to do, and so to identify their behavior as dropout in the narrow sense (that is, as failure) is both inaccurate and misleading — inaccurate because such a definition misrepresents their intentions, and misleading because it distorts the meaning they attach to their actions. It also distorts the educational goals of many colleges and programs that seek either to provide for those limited educational experiences or to encourage individuals to transfer to higher levels of the educational system.

Whatever the character of their personal goals, some students will alter them during their college careers, either because of maturation or the impact of the college experience. Although some of these individuals come to understand that higher education generally (or that which occurs in a particular institution) is not for them, this realization is in no direct sense a failure of intent. For some, it may signal a more realistic and mature determination of their needs, long-term interests, and the types of activities that lead to fulfillment; for others, it may reflect a realization that previously held goals were not in their best interests and that more time and varying experiences will be required to determine those interests. In either instance, it is not surprising that many persons withdraw from institutions to transfer to others, or that many persons simply suspend participation until a later time. To label these leaving behaviors as dropout in the sense of failure is, in effect, to deny the importance of both intellectual maturation and the hoped-for impact that college is deemed to have upon maturing individuals.

All this assumes, of course, that individuals enter college with clearly defined goals. In fact, this is not the case. A surprisingly large percentage of students entering college have little clear idea of why they are there, nor have they given serious thought to the choice of institution. For many high school graduates, the process of choosing a college is shockingly haphazard, often based on the scantiest of information. Little wonder, then, that, early in their college careers, so many students come to question the reasons for their being involved in higher education. The process of goal clarification will invariably lead some individuals either to withdraw from higher education altogether or to transfer to other institutions or programs, and this will likely be the case whether or not the institution invests heavily in career counseling for undergraduates.

The problem of defining dropout from the individual perspective is therefore more complex than simply noting the goals and/or intentions with which the person entered the higher educational system; it also entails determining that a person's experiences at a given institution are seen by that person as a failure to do or complete what he or she came to the institution to do. It is in this sense that the term "dropout" is best applied, for it is in this sense that there is a commonality of interest between the individual who enters college and the external observers who seek to increase retention in higher education. For institutional officials, in particular, such failure represents a failure of the institution, a failure to help the individual achieve what he or she initially set out to do.

Elements in the Process of Individual Dropout

From the individual point of view, then, dropping out means the failure to complete a given course of action or attain a desired goal for which he or she first entered a particular institution of higher education. As such, dropping out is dependent not only on individual intentions but also on the social and intellectual processes by which individuals come to realize desired goals within particular higher educational settings. Although a great variety of forces affect these processes, it is still true that individuals are largely responsible for attaining desired goals within the institution.

At the outset, it is necessary to recognize that individual drive, motivation, and skill are important parts of the attainment process. It simply takes effort to complete college. It is a regrettable but, perhaps, unavoidable fact of mass higher education that a number of students simply do not care enough or have the character to do what is required to complete a desired course of study. Some individuals are not sufficiently committed either to completing college or to putting forth the effort to attain that goal. For them, dropping out is more a result of not caring than it is of not being able to meet the demands of college work (Hackman and Dysinger, 1970).

But even with sufficient commitment, meeting academic standards and attaining higher educational goals require a range of adult intellectual and social skills that are of a higher level and more complex than those called for in high school. It is becoming increasingly evident that not all individuals who gain entry to institutions of higher education possess those skills. The absence, for instance of basic writing and mathematics skills among college students has been an issue of much recent concern among college officials. Nevertheless, although educators continue to measure and treat the absence of intellectual skills as if this absence alone were responsible for dropout, evidence abounds that social skills are equally important to persistence in college. These skills enable the person to locate, interact with, and use the resources for attainment (for example, students, faculty, and staff) available to students within the institution. The absence of social skills, especially among the disadvantaged segment of the student body, appears particularly important in the failure to maintain adequate levels of academic performance in college.

In any event, only some dropouts from higher education occur because of inadequate academic performance; most dropouts are voluntary. Individuals who withdraw from college often show levels of academic performance that exceed those of the students who persist. Rather than arising primarily from inadequate skills, such withdrawals appear to arise from incomplete personal integration into the intellectual and social mainstream of institutional life (Tinto, 1975). Evidence continues to mount that voluntary withdrawal is marked both by the holding of values incongruent with those that characterize the social and intellectual climates of the institution and by low levels of personal interaction with faculty members and other students, especially outside the formal classrooms and offices of the college (Pascarella and Terenzini,

1977). By the same token, the intellectual and social stimulation that proceeds from such interactions appears to be an essential component of the process by which individuals are able to meet their educational goals.

The Group- and Time-Variable Character of Dropout

The character of the dropout process is not invariable across student populations, nor is it uniform across college careers. Although such variations have been largely ignored in past research, it is now becoming clear that there may be significant differences between groups and across time in the process of dropping out from college. While much work has been done to reveal the multiple associations between rates of dropout and the attributes of individuals (for example, sex, race, ability, and social origins), virtually no attention has been given to the possibility that the longitudinal process of dropping out may itself vary among different groups of students (for example, between blacks and whites). Yet we know from other areas of educational research that significant differences do exist among groups for other forms of educational behavior. For instance, we have now begun to map out differences in the process of educational and status attainment that occur between blacks and whites and between males and females. For blacks (versus whites) and for females (versus males), it appears that educational attainment is more determined by social origins. Conversely, for whites and males status attainment is more influenced by individual ability. That this is true for the general process of educational attainment is particularly revealing, since it can be argued that the process of dropping out is in many respects its mirror image.

Fortunately, we do have some information pointing to a number of possible differences in the dropout processes that characterize different groups of college students. For instance, it seems evident that minority students face distinct problems in making contact with and establishing social and academic membership in largely majority institutions. For them, elements of social and academic integration, such as those that may arise through personal interaction with other students and with faculty members appears to be relatively more important to their persistence than they are for majority students. Interestingly, the feeling of not being marginal to (and therefore being integrated into the mainstream of) institutional life seems to characterize the experiences both of successful intervention programs and of persisting individuals of minority and/or disadvantaged backgrounds. The same conclusion may also apply to the experiences of adult learners in largely youthful student environments (Boshier, 1973); so, too, may it hold for commuting students in largely residential campuses, whose opportunities for personal interaction with other students and faculty can be quite limited. In either case, evidence suggests that on any campus there are groups of students who face distinct problems in accomplishing what they came to do, problems that require specific forms of intervention, as well as particular research methodologies to illuminate the characteristic persistence/dropout process.

As I have stated, evidence suggests that the dropout process also varies across college careers. The character of early college dropout is generally quite different from dropout occurring in the later years. Dropout is not only more frequent in the first years of college, but also more likely to be voluntary. This is true because difficulties in establishing contact with and achieving membership in the social and intellectual communities of the college tend to be greater very early in the college career than in the later years. For many individuals, the transition from the relatively small, local, and knowable climate of high school can be quite difficult. It simply takes some students time to adjust to the more adult world of college and develop the sorts of skills appropriate to the problems of membership in the college community. For certain students, the adjustment is extremely difficult, if not disabling. As a result, dropout in the form of voluntary withdrawal is more prevalent in the first several months following college entry.

Difficulty in making the transition to college occurs not only for the typical student who moves from a small high school to a larger college, where he or she may reside away from home, but also for other students, to whom the college experience may be entirely foreign, a remote part of their day-to-day activities. This problem applies to nontypical college students as well as to foreign students. "Nontypical" students include not only students of disadvantaged and/or minority backgrounds, but also those who go to college part-time while holding full-time jobs and those of more mature age who reenter the higher educational system after a number of years away from schooling. Research has shown the great importance of integration to the continued persistence of minority and/or disadvantaged students, and it is also true that making contact with the alien world of more youthful colleagues is equally important to the continuance of adult learners, who are now returning to college campuses in record numbers.

Dropout From the Institutional Perspective

Defining dropout from the institutional perspective is in some respects a more simple task than defining it for the individual. In other respects, however, it is considerably more difficult. It is more simple in the sense that all persons who withdraw from an institution of higher education can, regardless of their reasons for doing so, be classified as dropouts. Each withdrawal creates a vacancy in the student body that might have been filled by someone who would have persisted. Thus the departure of individuals can cause serious financial strains upon the host institution by undermining its continuing source of revenue. This is particularly evident in the private sector, where tuition charges are a substantial part of revenues, but it is no less a problem in the public sector when public revenues are scarce.

If this were the only consideration in defining dropout from the institutional perspective, the task of doing so would be quite simple. This is not the case, however, for it is not at all clear that all types of leaving behavior require equal attention or call for similar forms of action on the part of the institution. The difficult problem the institution faces in defining dropout is that of discerning which types of leaving behaviors, out of all those that may occur on campus, are to be considered dropout in the narrow sense and which types should be considered the normal outcome of institutional functioning. As noted above, disengagement behaviors arise from varying sources. A number are directly amenable to institutional action; others are not. Some forms of dropout may involve specific types of students, whose leaving may be of particular concern to institutional officials; other forms may entail the departure of individuals whose continued presence on campus may not be so important to the institution. Understanding these differences is both the beginning point of understanding dropout from the institutional perspective and the groundwork for developing effective institutional policies for student retention.

The Student Career and Institutional Dropout

From the institutional point of view, there are several critical periods in the student career when interactions between the institution and the individual most directly affect dropout. The first occurs during the application process, when the individual first makes contact with the institution. It is during the process of seeking out and applying for admission to a particular institution that first impressions are formed about the social and intellectual character of the institution. Such impressions, which arise in large measure from the printed materials the institution distributes to prospective students, are instrumental in the formation of preentry expectations about the nature of institutional life, and these expectations influence the quality of early interactions within the institution. The formation of unrealistic or mistaken expectations about the quality of student or academic life can lead to early disappointments and may set in motion a series of interactions leading to dropout. Thus it is in the institution's interest to develop among entering students realistic and accurate expectations as to the character of institutional life. Although the painting of a rosy picture via application materials may seem, in the short run, an effective way to increase the size of the applicant pool, in the long run it will only heighten dropout tendencies by increasing the gap between promise and delivery.

A second critical time in the student career is the period of transition between high school and college, which immediately follows entry to the institution. The first semester, especially the first six weeks, can be most difficult. This is particularly true at large, residential institutions, where individuals are often forced to make a transition from the relatively secure, knowable confines of small local high school communities (where students reside with their families) to a seemingly impersonal world, in which individuals have to fend for themselves, both in the classroom and in the dormitory. For many students, the speed and scale of the transition poses serious problems of adjustment, an adjustment not everyone is able to make independently. The sense of being "lost at sea," of not being able to make contact with other members of the institution, expresses in part the anomic situation in which many new students find themselves.

Not surprisingly, it is during this period of transition that dropout is most frequent, yet it is here that institutions can do much to prevent early dropout. Relatively simple interventions on the part of the institution can have an immediate and lasting impact upon student retention. The use of upper-class advisors, the holding of early advising and counseling sessions, the development of dormitory clusters, and the establishment of faculty stewardship for groups of new students are only a few of the possible interventions that can help individuals make the adjustment to college life.

The problem of making the transition to college is common to a variety of new students, not only to those moving from high school to large, residential campuses; it is no less important an issue, for example, among those institutions serving large numbers of nontraditional students. For the older learner returning to college, the transition between the adult world of home or work and the youthful domain of the campus can be quite traumatic. Transition problems can be equally severe for rural youth who attend large city universities and for individuals from minority and/or disadvantaged backgrounds who attend largely middle-class, majority institutions. For this last group, the social skills required for establishing membership in the majority culture of the institution are not part of the customary social repertoire, and becoming integrated into the social and academic mainstream of the institution is even more important for continued educational participation than it is for students from majority origins. By the same token, those institutional programs that are successful in keeping minority and/or disadvantaged students in college are precisely those that are able to provide for such integration (System Development Corporation, 1981).

Beyond the period of transition to college, dropout is most frequent in the later part of the first year and before the beginning of the second. While some dropouts arise from inability to meet academic demands, most of this later dropout is voluntary. Often it leads to transfer to other institutions of higher education rather than to permanent withdrawal from all forms of educational participation. The sources of such behavior are many. Some individuals find the demands of academic life unsuited to their own interests and tastes; others find it difficult to establish membership in the intellectual and social life of the institution; still others decide they would rather not establish such membership, if only because they find those communities unsuited to their own values and social preferences. While a number of individuals are unable to decide how they should direct their energies and resources, others decide that college completion is not for them.

Institutional Choice and Institutional Action

Clearly, no single intervention strategy will suffice. An institution must choose not only a course of action to pursue but also the types of leaving behavior it will seek to treat. Institutions can take several steps to deal with dropout. For instance, they can develop more effective career counseling early in the student career. They can also work to integrate the activities of the offices of admission, counseling, advising, and student services and thus ease the transition from high school to college. Efforts might also be made to develop institutionwide retention programs and/or to promote forms of organization restructuring that enhance the interaction of students and faculty members both within and outside the classroom. Extracurricular contact is especially important in the first year of college, when integration is a major concern of new students. In this regard, it is ironic that classes are frequently largest in the first year of college and often taught by graduate students, when the need for personal contact with other students and with faculty members is greatest.

Whatever the possible courses of action, it is not necessarily true that disengagement is equally deserving of institutional concern. For some students (for instance, those who find the communities of the campus unsuited to their own tastes), it may not be in the interest of either the institution or the individual to encourage persistence. The same possibility may also apply to individuals who perceive leaving as a positive step toward goal completion; for many such students, it may be in the interest of both parties for the institution to assist their transfer to other institutions and/or activities. This is not true, however, for those students whose goals are compatible with the institution's. For these persons, especially those who find it difficult to meet academic demands or who are having trouble making contact with and becoming integrated into the intellectual and social communities of the college, institutional intervention may prove fruitful. Whether assistance takes the form of academic or social counseling, the continued persistence of these individuals is in the interest of both parties. Conversely, the failure of these students is equally a failure of the institution.

From the institutional perspective, then, the question of defining dropout evolves into the question of choice — namely, discerning which among the many forms of attrition are worthy of action. All forms of leaving can be labelled dropout, but they are not all equally deserving of policy action, and no institution can possibly seek to attend to all forms of disengagement. The actions an institution takes to deal with some forms of dropout are likely to constrain its ability to deal with other forms. Ultimately, the institution's task is to define dropout in terms of educational as well as institutional goals. It must be mindful that it is educating and not merely schooling its students.

The Variable Character of Dropout Among Institutions

Institutions differ in their goals as well as in their student bodies, and their definitions of dropout also vary. While much of this variation necessarily reflects the particular circumstances of individual institutions, some variations reflect differences between types or categories of institutions. Among two-year institutions, for example, dropout as transfer may be seen as an understandable and even desirable form of attrition, while the same behavior at elite, private colleges may be viewed as a serious problem. Similarly, academic dismissal at open-enrollment institutions may be of little concern, but at academically competitive institutions such dismissals may be of direct concern to institutional officials. Each dropout may be a source of worry to institutions that accept virtually everyone who applies (over 50 percent of all institutions of higher education), but dropout may be of less consequence to those highly selective instituitions that admit only a few applicants (10 percent of all institutions).

Differences among institutions may also help account for the varying frequency of different types of dropout behaviors. For instance, as it relates to the occurrence of voluntary withdrawal, students at small colleges may experience very different problems in establishing membership within the institution than do students at large universities. Small colleges may enhance the likelihood of frequent student–faculty and student–student interaction, but restrict the range of possible student communities of subcultures in which to establish membership. Social and intellectual integration may then be more difficult for individuals who have disparate or deviant social and intellectual orientations. This is less likely to be true at very large institutions, where the range or student subcultures is bound to be greater, but larger schools may limit the opportunities for student–faculty contacts outside the classroom. In the smaller colleges then, dropout may arise more often from value or social incongruity, while in much larger institutions it may result more often from insufficient social and intellectual interactions with faculty members.

Dropout From the State and National Perspective

The question of dropout changes markedly once we move away from the perspective of the individual institution to that of higher levels of educational organization. From the perspective of the state, for instance, dropout as transfer among state institutions may not represent dropout in the narrow sense of the term, if it produces only internal transfers within the public sector. If, however, it creates movements to private institutions or out-of-state colleges, it is likely to be viewed as dropout, strictly speaking. In the same vein, at the national level, only those forms of institutional disengagement that lead to total withdrawal from any type of formal participation in higher education are likely to be considered dropouts. All other movements leading to institutional transfer may be seen as representing internal migration of students within the national system of higher education.

At higher levels of educational organization, therefore, it is important to distinguish between transfer and total withdrawal behaviors, and, among the former, between those transfers that take place within the public sector and/or within state and those that occur between the public and private sectors or lead to out-of-state movements. From those organizational perspectives, dropout occurs only when a person leaves and/or stops participating in any form of higher education under the jurisdiction of that organization. Other types of movements are likely to be viewed as forms of internal adjustments or migrations within domains of organization jurisdiction. As a result, the concern of higher-level educational officials lies both in the control and fine-tuning of internal movements and in the reduction, if possible, of student departure from their educational organizations.

Differing perspectives on dropout lead, in turn, to different ways of analyzing and explaining its occurrence. Generally, we find an emphasis less on individual movements and the role of individual attributes therein than on aggregate movements of individuals and the role of institutional and aggregate-level phenomena in their patterning. For instance, the perspective of the state- or national-level official could give rise to an analysis of patterns of student migration that parallels that of state and national labor officials who study the movement of labor among states and industries within their region. The models of migration that emphasize the effect of "push" and "pull" factors on labor movement might also be applied to the problem of student migration. For example, in the same fashion that varying employment requirements are used in labor migration studies, the existence of differing admission standards could be employed in the study of student migration among institutions. Whether applied to all students generally or to the migration of differing groups of students, these modes of analysis can give rise to retention policies markedly different from those normally applied by individual institutions. One such policy could entail the systematic use of differential tuition pricing to influence the movements of students among differing institutions by altering the relative pricing of competing educational offerings. The same effect could be obtained generally (or for particular groups of students) by the differential distribution of financial aid, which would alter the costs to the individual of attending particular institutions.

Limits of State and National Policies for Student Retention

Not all movements within or outside regions of educational control are so easily amenable to higher-level educational policies. Some students move among institutions and/or regions for reasons that have little to do with issues of pricing. Climate, both institutional and ecological, may be important considerations for some students, while for others, nearness to home may be more important. Policies that may be effective in altering the migration of some groups of students may be counterproductive or useless in affecting the movement of other groups.

In any event, there are common societal forces that also limit the effectiveness of state and national retention efforts. These forces underlie and shape the very inclination to attend and persist in higher education, in ways which are not easily amenable to regional or national action. The effect of such forces can be seen, for instance, in a very simple time-series analysis of aggregate rates of four-year college completion in the nation as a whole over the past 100 years (Tinto, forthcoming). The plot of those rates over time reveals two striking features. First, with the exception of one period, rates of completion (dropout) have remained strikingly constant at about 55 (45) percent over the past 100 years, and this has been true despite drastic changes during that time, both in the character of higher education and in the number and types of students participating. This is a period also marked most recently by a range of state and national policies aimed at increasing both entry into and persistence within the system of an increasing number of students. Second, the one period of noticeable change in rates of persistence (dropout) is the one that occurred during and immediately following World War II. Rates of college completion understandably decreased during the war and increased immediately afterward (until 1952). Credit has been given to the G.I. Bill for the return to college of many veterans, but the increase in completion rates after the war almost perfectly matches the decrease in rates that occurred during the war. Rather than increasing the overall proportion of persons who obtained college degrees over the twelve-year period from 1940 to 1952, the G.I. Bill seems to have enabled those who initially entered college during the war to reenter afterward; it does not appear to have increased college completion among persons who otherwise would not have gone to college after completing high school.

Conclusions

The study of dropout from higher education is extremely complex, for it involves not only a variety of perspectives but also a range of differeing types of dropout behavior. No one definition of dropout is likely to capture entirely the complexity of its appearance in higher education. Researchers and institutional officials have to choose with some care the definitions that best suit their interests and goals. In so doing, they should recall the primary goal for which higher education exists — namely, the education (not simply the schooling) of individuals. Retention without reference to its educative consequences is in the interests of neither individuals nor institutions.

References

Boshier, R. "Educational Participation and Dropout: A Theoretical Model." *Adult Education,* 1973, *23* (4), 255–282.

Hackman, J., and Dysinger, W. S. "Commitment to College as a Factor in Student Attrition." *Sociology of Education,* 1970, *43* (3), 311–324.

Pascarella, E. T., and Terenzini, P. "Patterns of Student–Faculty Informal Interaction Beyond the Classroom and Voluntary Freshman Attrition." *Journal of Higher Education,* 1977, *48* (5), 540–562.

System Development Corporation. *Progress Report on the Evaluation of Special Services in Higher Education.* Santa Monica: System Development Corporation, 1981.

Tinto, V. "Dropout from Higher Education: A Theoretical Synthesis of Recent Research." *Review of Educational Research,* 1975, *43* (1), 89–125.

Tinto, V. "Student Disengagement Revisited: Some Thoughts on the Limits of Theory and Practice in Student Attrition." *The Journal of Higher Education* (forthcoming).

Vincent Tinto is an associate professor of sociology and education at Syracuse University. He has carried out research and consulted and written extensively in the field of higher education, especially on the issues of inequality, dropout, and the impact of schooling upon adult occupational success.

In the 1960s, the lack of theoretical models of student attrition
was loudly decried. In the 1970s, several were proposed, and
now the institutional reseacher has the opportunity to choose
from among them.

Conceptual Models of Student Attrition: How Theory Can Help the Institutional Researcher

John P. Bean

Theories and Models

Theories often have a bad reputation among practitioners. They are seen as too abstract, difficult to understand, and not really applicable to the particular case at hand. Another opinion is that there is nothing more practical than a good theory, and that is the point of view proposed in this chapter.

Kerlinger (1973, p. 9) provides us with a technical definition of *theory.* He writes, "A theory is a set of interrelated constructs (concepts), definitions, and propositions that present a systematic view of phenomena by specifying relationships among variables, with the purpose of explaining and predicting the phenomena." In simple terms, a theory explains why things happen and in the explanation describes some aspect of the world around us. A theory of student attrition describes the attrition process — it explains why students drop out of school. In another way, a theory of student attrition can be used to predict which students are most likely to drop out of school. Theory guides research. It tells us what variables or constructs we should focus on in a study and how those variables are related to what we are trying to explain. It also helps us by eliminating variables that cannot be deduced from the theory.

Theory is not a panacea. Its value lies in its usefulness for explaining

E. Pascarella (Ed.). *New Directions for Institutional Research: Studying Student Attrition*, no. 36. San Francisco: Jossey-Bass, December 1982.

why things happen and for guiding the selection of certain constructs (variables) and the elimination of others. Thorngate (1976) identified the tradeoffs in using different types of theories. Theories of social behavior are simple, general, accurate, or a combination of two of these factors, but not simultaneously all three.

Models. A model is a simplified version of reality, in which the minutiae and detail are stripped away, leaving what are assumed to be important factors in the study of something and the interrelationships among these factors. A model forms a bridge between a purely abstract theory and the practical solution to a question. The structure of a theoretical model is usually deduced from theory, while the content of the model is often derived inductively (that is, from empirical study). Thus the theory is taken from the level of abstraction to the level of concreteness. Theory construction, model building, and observation are reciprocal and circular processes, each feeding on the other two.

Models are important because they tie theory to specific situations. Models are intentionally practical. While a theory can be refuted by a single exception, a model can be retained for as long as it is useful. The practical function of models of student attrition is what makes them so important to institutional researchers.

Models of Student Attrition

A model of student attrition is a representation of the factors presumed to influence decisions to drop out of an institutions. The model identifies the interrelationships among the various factors and the relationships between these factors and the dropout decision. The first important issue faced by researchers is defining dropout; as Vincent Tinto has shown in Chapter One of this volume, the issue is not trivial.

Once a researcher has decided upon a definition of dropout, he or she is left with the decision of what variables to measure and what model of relationships among the variables to use. The use of any model is based on certain assumptions about what is important in a dropout decision at a particular institution. The rest of this chapter will discuss six types of models, all of which have the potential to help us understand the attrition process.

Atheoretical Models: The Descriptive Studies. Descriptions are based on observed facts. Factual statements are empirical generalizations, that is, things or relationships are assumed to exist because they are seen to exist. In an atheoretical (or descriptive) study, empirical generalizations are made about the characteristics of dropout (for example, 60 percent of the freshmen who drop out are commuters; 25 percent of the freshment who drop out have a B average; 35 percent of the students who drop out are minorities). These statements represent correlation among variables, not causation. From these statements, an institutional researcher can describe the extent of attrition, the time when students are most likely to drop out, and selected characteristics of dropouts (for example, high school grades, standardized test scores, majors, sex, age, race, and so forth). What one cannot do from a descriptive study is say why a student is likely to drop out of an institution, but a descriptive study is not a waste of time and as a first step can be valuable in generating propositions to be examined in a second study. Descriptive studies are atheoretical because they are not based on a theory that links the variables in the study. Linkages (correlations) may be established, but the reasons why variables are related is not specified.

Prematriculation Characteristics. The second framework for the analysis of student attrition comes from studies that have looked at the input characteristics of students and on this basis have attempted to predict the likelihood that a student will stay at a given institution. One approach here has been to produce more atheoretical studies attempting to identify those factors that would best predict which students would stay and which would drop out. In general, these factors have fallen into three catagories — academic, demographic, and financial factors (Lenning, Beal, & Sauer, 1980). Again, one is left with the correlates of attrition, that is, factors that vary with levels of attrition. An explanation of why these factors work is still lacking. The value of such studies is like that of other atheoretical studies, but their outcomes focus on strategies for admission, not on strategies for retention. If it is found that students with high class rankings are more likely to stay in school once they have matriculated, an institution might attempt to attract and admit students who rank high in their high school classes. Again, the simplicity of the research is very attractive, but such a finding does not explain why, for example, some students who ranked very high in their high school classes dropped out of college.

Rootman (1972): Person–Role Fit. Models using the theory of person-role fit focus on the relationship between characteristics of the individual and the requirements of the student role at a particular institution. As we shall see, these models are complementary to the Tinto (1975) and Spady (1970) models, which focus on academic and social integration — namely, a student with a high level of person–role fit would be likely to have a high level of academic and social integration in an institution.

Rootman (1972) studied freshman attrition at the U.S. Coast Guard Academy. He used a very wide range of indicators to come up with what is essentially a simple causal model of voluntary withdrawal from a total adult socializing organization. In this case, voluntary student withdrawal from the organization is viewed as a result of the failure of the adult socialization process. Rootman used a person–role-fit model derived from the work of Biddle and Thomas (1966).

Rootman's model may be simplified such that two independent variables have positive direct effects on voluntary withdrawal and two have negative effects. Discussing leaving with outsiders and discussing leaving with insiders are both positively related to attrition. These seem similar in effect to intent to leave, in the sense that they may at least partially represent the notion of a self-fulfilling prophecy (Merton, 1968). The second two variables are actual interpersonal fit and person–role fit, which are negatively associated with voluntary withdrawal. Rootman's operationalization of these two variables is similar to the academic and social-integration variables that have appeared in other models. Here, actual interpersonal fit is similar to friendship support, and person–role fit is similar to shared group values. Proceeding from a largely empirical theoretical base, Rootman's findings are consistent with the model proposed by Spady (1970).

To conduct a study using a person–role fit strategy, a researcher would want to focus on characteristics of the individual student and simultaneously develop a profile of what the student role actually is at the institution. The characteristics of the student are psychological, and their delineation would require one or more psychological tests. The definition of the student role at an institution is extremely complex. This complexity arises in part because there is not just one student role at an institution, and individual perception of the student role is probably more important to the individual than is any abstract definition of student role. To gather data for such a study, an institutional researcher would need to obtain questionnaire data from students before matriculation and again after students have had an opportunity to develop a sense of what the student role is at the institution. The higher the level of similarity between student characteristics (for example, high need for achievement) and student role (for example, students are expected to be highly competitive), the more likely the student would be to stay.

The person–role-fit strategy is probably not the most useful one for institutional researchers, primarily because an institution, particularly during the 1980s, may have little control over the personality types of the students who matriculate. The theory is simple and general and can therefore be expected to lack accuracy (Thorngate, 1976). The costs for such a study would include the preparation, printing, distribution, and collection of two different questionnaires and the compilation and analysis of the data. The outcomes should provide information about the admission of certain types of students who do not have the characteristic of students who are likely to stay or information about the modification of expectations for students, so that the students who actually have matriculated would meet the set of expectations for the institution's student role.

The Longitudinal-Process Models (Spady, Tinto, Pascarella)

Spady (1970): The First Theoretical Model of the Dropout Process. Spady (1970) selectively borrowed Durkheim's (1961) idea that shared group values and friendship support are expected to reduce suicide and, by analogy, dropout. This theory forms the foundation for the Spady (1970), Tinto (1975), and Pascarella (1980) models, in which social and academic integration, which correspond to shared group values and friendship support, are both expected to influence the dropout decesion. Spady's explanatory sociological model of the dropout process (1970) constitutes the first full-blown theoretical model. In his model, shared group values, grade performance, normative congruence, and friendship support were expected to lead to increased social integration. Social integration was expected to increase satisfaction, which was expected in turn to increase institutional commitment. Institutional commitment reduced the likelihood of dropping out.

Several characteristics of this model merit discussion. To begin with, Spady specified that dropout decisions are the result of a longitudinal process. Secondly, he identified background characteristic as important in the dropout process—specifically, family background, academic potential, ability, and socio-economic status. Next, directly from Durkheim (1961), he identified normative congruence and friendship support as important variables in his model. To these he added the college-specific variables of grade performance and intellectual development. This model indicated that all these factors lead to greater social integration. Social integration was expected to increase satisfaction, and satisfaction in turn would increase institutional commitment, which was the direct antecedent of dropout. In addition, grade performance (because a student can flunk out of school) could be expected to have a direct effect on attrition. In this case, institutional commitment was operationalized in Spady's (1971) empirical study by a question that asked the extent of the student's hopes to graduate from the university in question.

Tinto (1975): A Synthetic Model Based on Recent Literature. Tinto (1975) produced what is the most widely cited model of the student attrition process and the most widely tested in empirical studies (see Pascarella, 1980). This work is highly congruent with the work of Durkheim (1961) and Spady (1970). In this model, background characteristics (including family background, individual attributes, and precollege schooling) interact with each other and are expected to influence both goal commitment (commitment to the goal of graduation) and institutional commitment (See Figure 1). In the academic system, goal commitment leads to higher grade performance and intellectual development, which lead in turn to academic integation, which, in circular fashion, leads to even greater goal commitment. Goal commitment reduces the likelihood of dropping out. In the social system, institutional commitment is expected to produce peer group and faculty interaction, which leads to social integration, which in turn increases institutional commitment. Institutional commitment is also expected to reduce the likelihood of dropping out.

This model is more linear than Spady's model, but contains basically the same elements. The chief conceptual problem of the model is the placement of goal commitment and institutional commitment twice in the model. The first type of goal commitment seems to be the product of prematriculation characteristics, and the second seems to be the product of academic integration. At any particular point in a student's career, however, he or she will have a single notion of goal commitment, which is expected to be the product of both prematriculation characteristics and academic and social integration— that is, experience modifies attitudes. One would expect that the latter set of

Figure 1.

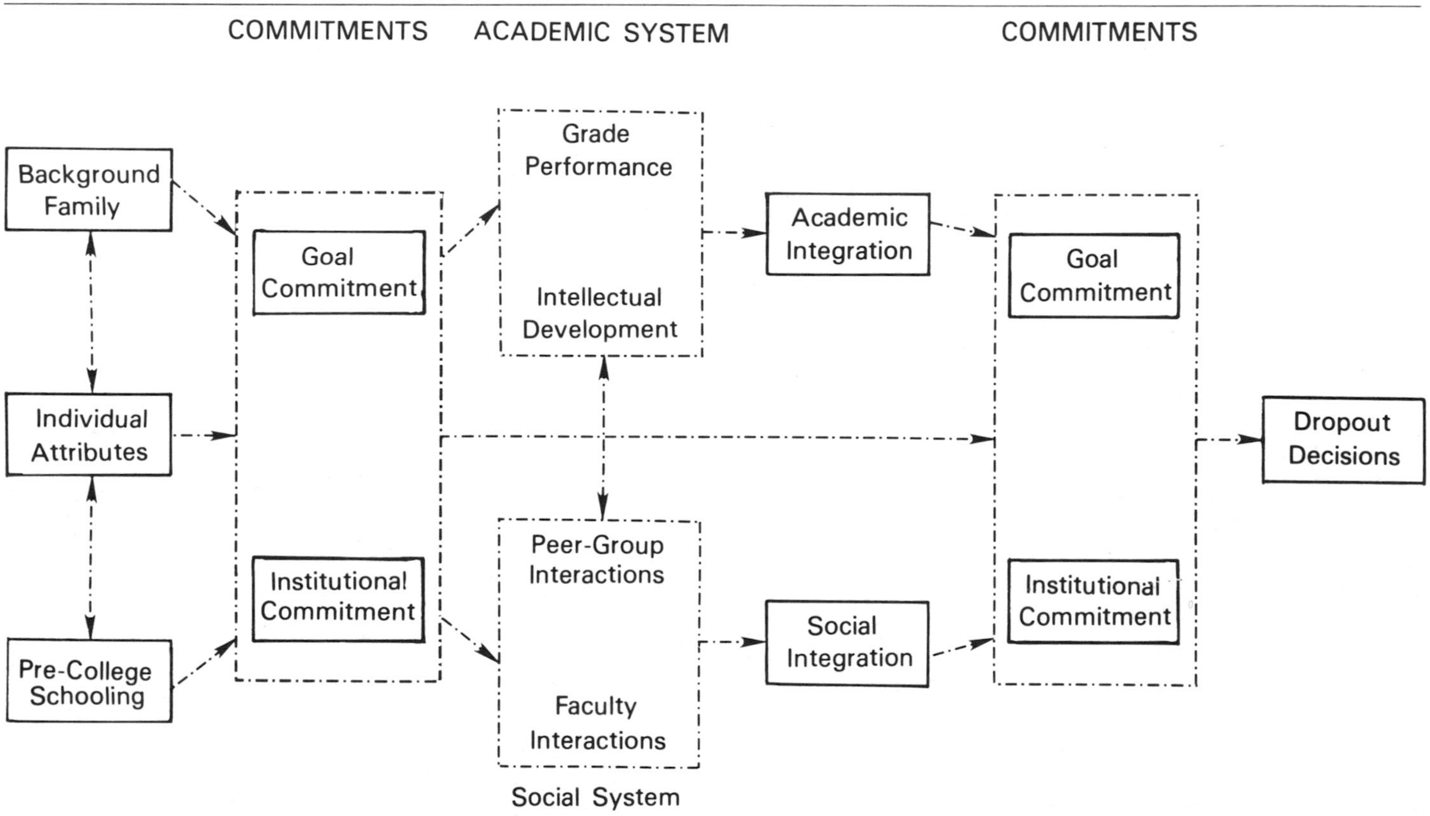

goal commitments, not the initial set, would be the best predictors of dropout decision. The initial goal commitments and institutional commitments seem to be qualitatively different from the latter—namely, they are educational plans, rather than the commitment to carrying out those plans. This commitment comes from a student's interaction with the institution.

Pascarella (1980): Student–Faculty Informal Contact. Pascarella (1980) has developed a conceptual model of the dropout process emphasizing the importance for students of informal contact with faculty members. In his model, background characteristics are expected to interact with institutional image, administrative policies and decisions, size, admissions, academic standards, and so forth. These institutional factors are expected to influence informal contact with faculty members, other college experiences (for example, peer culture, classes, and extracurricular and leisure activities), and educational outcomes (for example, academic performance, intellectual development, personal development, educational and career aspirations, college satisfaction, and institutional integration). Educational outcomes are expected to directly influence persistence/withdrawal decisions. Background characteristics are expected to have a direct influence on institutional factors, informal contact with faculty, other college experiences, and educational outcome. Informal contact with faculty is expected to influence other college experiences and be influenced by these. Informal contact with faculty is also supposed to influence educational outcomes and be influenced by these.

These three models have at least three things in common. First of all, they describe attrition as a longitudinal process: The background characteristics of a student influence the way in which the student interacts with the college environment, which leads to educational and attitudinal outcomes, which in turn culminate in a decision to stay in or drop out of school. Second, each model finds as its theoretical base the social and academic integration of the student with the institution, a theory developed by Durkheim (1961) to explain differences in the rate of suicide among various segments of European society. Third, each model is complex. These theories have given up simplicity to increase accuracy and, to some extent, generalizability. The extent to which the models can be generalized depends to a great extent on how research using these models is operationalized—specifically, whether questions relating to academic and social integration are specific to an institution or more general.

Studies based on such models could be expected to provide at least two very important pieces of information. First, an institutional researcher should be able to tell whether entry-level characteristics or institutional characteristics are more important in influencing dropout decisions. This would tell the institution if it should spend more of its resources recruiting students who have better chances of staying at the institution until graduation or if it should spend more on programs related to those factors that keep people in school. Second, an institutional researcher should be able to tell whether academic or social factors contribute most to a student's leaving and suggest that resources be allocated accordingly to reduce attrition. The overall value of such a study is that the institution should begin to be able to identify some of the reasons why students leave, not just the characteristics of leavers.

Bean (in press): An Industrial Model of Student Attrition. A model developed by Price and Mueller (1981) was adapted for Bean's study (in press) of student attrition. The adapted model contained ten variables, which reflected the student's interaction with the institution (grades, practical value of the education received, the sense of self-development due to schooling, the repetitiveness of school life, information related to the student role, participation in decision making, having close friends, having the courses one wants to take, being treated fairly, and memberships in campus organizations). These variables were all expected to influence satisfaction, which in turn was expected to decrease intent to leave. Intent to leave is positively related to dropout. In addition, two variables external to the organization—opportunity to transfer and likelihood of marrying—were directly and positively related to intent to leave and dropout. Variables similar to academic and social-integration variables in Tinto's and Spady's models appear among the variables of interaction with the institution; also among these variables are several attitudinal variables.

Using the variables found in this model, Bean was able to describe about 50 percent of the variance in dropout in a single institution. Part of the success of the model is due to the attitudinal variables and intent to leave. Another important contribution of this model is the operationalization of specific elements within the person–role fit and the social-integration variables of Rootman's and Spady's models. Because of the importance of intent to leave, the work of Fishbein and Ajzen (1975) is crucial to continued development of the synthetic model.

Fishbein and Ajzen (1975): The Importance of Intentions in Influencing Behavior. The basic Fishbein and Ajzen model indicates that behavior is preceded by an intention to perform the behavior (see Figure 2). The immediate antecedents of intent to perform the behavior are attitude toward the behavior and a subjective norm concerning the behavior. Beliefs about the consequences of a behavior precede the attitude toward the behavior, and normative beliefs about a behavior influence the subjective norm concerning the behavior. A feedback loop from the behavior itself to these beliefs completes the model. Thus the attitude and the subjective norm about a behavior lead to intention to perform or not to perform the behavior, which in turn leads to the behavior itself. Bentler and Speckart (1979) add another variable to this process, that of past behavior. In their model, past behavior, attitude, and a subjective norm all lead to intentions to perform a behavior, followed by actual performance of the behavior. Thus attitudes, norms, and past behavior directly influence intention, and all four variables directly influence future behavior.

According to this model, dropout decisions at a university should be the result of past behavior, attitudes, and norms, with intent as an intervening variable. Intent replaces institutional commitment as the immediate precursor of dropout decisions. Both the Spady and Tinto models have institutional

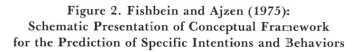

Figure 2. Fishbein and Ajzen (1975):
Schematic Presentation of Conceptual Framework
for the Prediction of Specific Intentions and Behaviors

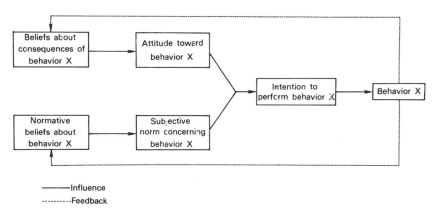

commitment as the last endogenous variable before dropout. In the research of Bean (1980, 1981), intent to leave has been the best predictor of attrition, which lends credence to the Fishbein and Ajzen model. Johnson (1980) also reports such findings. The primary value of intent as a variable is for prediction of attrition, however, and not in the explanation of the factors that cause attrition. When attrition is highly correlated with intentions, the problem for the researcher is to explain intentions.

The Synthetic Model

Various elements taken from models discussed above can be synthesized into a single model of student attrition (see Figure 3). It should be remembered that the purpose of this model is not a full explanation of the dropout process across institutions or at the national level; instead, it indicates the information about a student that, if it were known, would likely indicate that student's probability of dropping out and some of the reasons why. The synthetic model identifies four classes of variables — background variables, organizational variables, environmental variables, and attitudinal and outcome variables — that all have direct or indirect effects on intent to leave, which is the immediate precursor of dropping out. This model allows researchers to identify classes of variables related in a causal sequence. Variables can be added to or deleted from the model to suit the particular needs of an institution. Table 1 indicates how variables taken from the models discussed in this paper, in the author's previous work, and in the major reviews of the literature (cited above) would be placed in the model. A discussion of the model follows.

Background Variables. Background variables represent facts about students who have not yet entered college. These variables precede the student's interaction with the organization or an assessment of the organizational envir-

Figure 3. A Synthetic Causal Model of Student Attrition

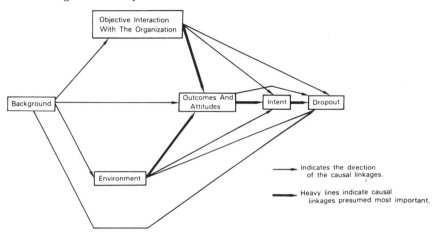

onment as the student's college career proceeds. They are included largely to enhance the explanation of organizational variables and environmental variables and are of practical use to admissions committees. These variables can be used to indicate the types of problems an institution can expect when admitting students with certain attributes. Such variables generally contribute little to the explained variance of dropout when information is known about organizational, environmental, and attitudinal variables and intent to leave (Bean, 1980, 1981). The most important of these variables is probably performance (high school grades and ACT scores), which predicts from about 25 to 50 percent of the variance in college grades.

These background variables do not contain attitudinal assessments, but only indicate facts. There are two reasons for this. First, if one knew the educational goals of the student *after* he or she had entered an institution, this information would undoubtedly be more important than initial or prematriculation educational goals in predicting dropout. Prematriculation educational goals would probably be related to the educational goals of the student once enrolled, but it is this secondary assessment of educational goals that would be expected to affect a dropout decision more profoundly. Second, respondents attending the institution could answer these questions without being asked to make assessments of the goals or values they had held prior to matriculation; thus a single instrument could be used to assess these background variables. If prematriculation attitudes are to be used as background variables, this information must be obtained before students enter the institution. It is important, nevertheless, to have these variables measured, so that one can control their effects statistically when assessing the influence of subsequent variables in the model.

Organizational Variables. The organizational variables are indicators of the student's interaction with the organization. They are intended to reflect the respondent's objective experience of the organization (for example the

Table 1. Variables Classified for Use in the
Synthetic Model of Student Attrition

Background Variables

*Mother's education
*Father's education
*High school grades
*Achievement test scores
 High school size
 Hometown size
 College preparatory curriculum
 Distance home
 State resident
 Head of household's occupation
 Parents' income
 Religion

Organizational Variables

 Regulation of life at school
 Repetitiveness of school
 Communication of policies
*Close friends
 Helpfulness of advisor
*Informal contact with faculty
*Grades
 Participation in decision making
*Memberships in campus organizations
*Curriculum (availability of
    preferred courses)
 Housing
 Job
 University services used
 Peer culture
 Leisure activities
 Financial aid
*Discussed leaving with outsiders
*Discussed leaving with insiders

Intentions

*Intent to leave

Environmental Variables

*Opportunity (transfer)
 Opportunity (job)
*Family approval (institution)
 Family approval (major)
 Family responsibilities
*Likelihood of marrying
 Difficulty of financing school
 Military draft
 Economic indicators (CPI index,
    employment rate)
 Social fads

Outcome and Attitudinal Variables

*Practical value
 Institutional quality
 Self-development
 Satisfaction
*Boredom
*Confidence
 Adjustment
*Certainty of choice
 Fairness of treatment
 Competitiveness of academic program
*Loyalty
*Major certainty
 Occupational certainty
*Educational goals
*Absenteeism

Variables for Statistical Control

 Age
 Ethnicity
 Year in school
 Full-time/Part-time status
 Transfer/Nontransfer
 U.S. citizenship
 Sex

*Presumed to have a greater influence on dropout than other variables in the category.

number of close friends, the amount of informal contact with the faculty, the amount of help an advisor gives in specified areas, membership in campus organizations, and so forth). These variables include the structural variables, that is, variables that can be administratively manipulated. For example, if informal contacts with faculty members reduce attrition, these contacts could be encouraged or required by the institution. If students who do not participate in decision making drop out of the institution at a high rate, student participation in decision making could be increased. As suggested by Bentler and Speckart (1979) and Locke (1976), it is these behaviors that will influence attitudes.

The organizational variables are also those variables by which one would determine the extent of students' sharing of group values, friendship support, and the regulation of behavior by institutions (Durkheim, 1961). It is here that variables should be placed indicating Spady's (1970) grade performance, normative congruence, friendship support, and social discussion with insiders and outsiders of leaving; Tinto's (1975) grade performance, peer group interaction, and faculty interaction; Price's (1977) pay (grades being a surrogate measure for pay), participation in decision making, repetitiveness, and communication; indicators of the extent to which students use any services provided by the university; and other institution-specific varialbes.

Environmental Variables. The environmental variables are structural opposites of the organizational variables — that is, they are variables over which the organization has little or no control. These include opportunity to transfer or get a job, family approval of the institution and the student's major, family responsibilities, the likelihood of marrying, and the difficulty of financing school. Lenning, Beal, and Sauer (1980) identified three other environmental variables — the military draft, economic cycles, and social forces. Some of the environmental variables (for example, opportunity to transfer, family responsibilities, and difficulty in financing school) may directly influence dropout, other variables (for example, family approval of the institution and the student's major) may have a greater influence on attitudinal variables such as institutional quality. This set of variables generally has not been classified as environmental and has not been widely studied (Bean 1978, 1980, 1981). Whereas most research is concentrated on what could push a student out of an institution, these variables indicate ways in which the student might be pulled from the institution. Again, they should reflect more or less objective assessments of the environment outside the educational institution. Of course, difficulty in financing school might be mitigated by the institution itself, but generally it would reflect parents' income or the accessibility of special loan programs provided by state or federal government sources.

Attitudinal and Outcome Variables. The attitudinal and outcome variables are expected to indicate more subjective evaluations of education, educational institution, and goals — a subjective interpretation of the objective educational experience. These variables include assessments of the practical value of one's education, the institution's quality, and one's own self-development; the satisfaction and boredom one feels at school; confidence in being a successful student; adjustment of the institution; certainty of choice in attending the institution; loyalty (the importance of graduating from this institution as opposed to some other); major; occupational certainty; and educational goals.

Absenteeism is also included in the model here (although being absent is not an attitude, but a behavior). These variables include some of what Pascarella (1980) considered educational outcomes and what Bean (1979) considered personal variables, and they certainly contain what Ajzen and Fishbein (1980) would call attitudes.

Some direct effects are possible from these variables on dropout. It is expected that most of these variables would have significant relationships with intent to leave, at least using a t-test. In multiple regression, multicolinearity and the sheer number of these attitudinal variables would make it difficult for all to be significantly and simultaneously related to intent to leave. It is suspected, however, that the attitudinal variables will subsume most of the direct effects of the organizational and environmental variables on intent to leave and that intent to leave would be better explained by these attitudinal variables than by others in the model. It should be noted that institutional commitment, important in the models of Spady and Tinto, is indicated here by the attitudinal variables of loyalty and certainty of choice.

Intent to Leave. Intent to leave is hypothesized to be the best predictor of dropout and to subsume most of the effects of the attitudinal, organizational, environmental, and background variables in explaining the variance in dropout. Its location in the model is well supported by the extensive research of Fishbein and Ajzen (1975), as well as by previous studies of student attrition (Bean, 1980, 1981; Johnson, 1980). The attitudinal variables are expected to be the best predictors of intent to leave, although environmental variables such as opportunity to transfer and organizational variables such as grades might also have direct effects on intent to leave. The location of intent to leave is also appropriate in the sense of Merton's (1968) notion of self-fulfilling prophecy. Thus the location of intent to leave in the model is supported by theoretical and empirical studies.

Rules for the Inclusion of New Variables in the Model. There are many variables that may be important to understanding dropout at a particular institution — for example, religious variables (at a religious college) or a local industry's attempts to hire students before graduation. As a practical matter, as well as to maintain the theoretical integrity of an empirical study, some rules about the placement of variables in the model should be established.

1. Background variables should probably include only objective information about a student before matriculation and attitudes, plans beliefs, and so forth, measured before matriculation.

2. Organizational variables should include only those variables that can be verified by observing a student or the student's record (for example, the length and frequency of out-of-class contacts with a faculty member, types of subjects discussed, number of memberships in campus organizations, the information a student has about rules and requirements, numbers of courses a student is closed out of, and so forth).

3. Environmental variables should include objective and subjective assessments of the student's environment — that is, anything not directly asso-

ciated with the organization or its members but relevant to the student's decision to remain in school. Opportunities to transfer and the military draft are obvious examples.

4. Attitudinal and outcome variables, by and large, represent the psychological results of interacting with an organization. They should include attitudes toward the institution, evaluations of the educational process and institutional policies, and similar outcomes. The location of absenteeism (as an outcome rather than an organizational variable) and grades (as an organizational rather than an outcome variable) is problematical. Grades are definitely an outcome of organizational interaction; yet, like pay in work organizations, they are an objective element in organizational-individual interactions. Absenteeism, an objective and observable element in organizational-individual interactions, is treated in the turnover literature as an immediate precursor of quitting. Final placement in the model will depend on further empirical tests or on the exact question a researcher has about grades or absenteeism.

Because this model is derived from a more general theoretical base, it can be applied to any type of institution with (one would expect) similar results. Because institutions differ in their characteristics, however, the selection of variables for a questionnaire would undoubtedly be based on local conditions: If no one lives in fraternity houses, it would be silly to ask questions about one, and if 50 percent of the student body works part-time for a local industry, it would be equally unwise to ignore that fact.

Since studies using the synthetic model (for example, Bean, 1981) include an intent variable, this type of study is valuable not only in explaining the attrition process but also in identifying potential dropouts before they leave. Thus such studies can be used to identify students who show high potential for leaving an institution and can also be used to explain the attrition process at a particular school.

Data for such studies can come from a single questionnaire, but this provides only information related to intent to leave, not actual attrition. It is advisable to add data from student records, so that attrition and not just intent to leave will be studied. Intent is not a perfect predictor of behavior and grows worse as time elapses between the measure of intentions and the expected behavior. Also, degree of certainty about one's intentions varies, and a number of responses may fall into the "probable" category. One could add to such studies information related to prematriculation characteristics from student records; information on the activities of the student while enrolled (courses, major, grades, and so forth); the registration status of the student (full-time versus part-time); and, for students who do not reenroll, information related to their activities after leaving school (for example, whether they transfer, drop out with no intention of pursuing higher education, or actually return at a later date).

The costs of such studies could vary tremendously, depending on the level of detail and the types of data used. If a single questionnaire is used, costs involve printing, distribution, collection, keypunching, and data analysis. More costs are incurred with the addition of each new type of data. Sample size has a direct influence on costs, but, using a random sample, one loses information about particular groups—for example, the analysis of business majors versus English majors versus undeclared students. If there are significant intergroup differences, then separate models could be developed for each group the results to be shared with particular colleges or departments.

Conclusions

Several models of student attrition have been presented in this chapter, each with some advantages and some limitations. Throughout the presentation, it has been suggested that theoretical studies are preferable to atheoretical studies if our objective it to discover why students are leaving institutions, not simply who is leaving. They are preferable because the field of study has developed to the point where descriptive studies abound. The time has come to link variables found in descriptive studies, using theory.

Before selecting a theory or a theoretical approach, an institutional researcher should have the purpose of an attrition study clearly in mind. Studies of attrition commonly focus on four issues: What are the reasons students leave school? Which students are likely to leave this institution this year (or semester)? What effect are our programs and services having on attrition? What are the entry-level characteristics of the students most likely to stay in school or to leave? For the first type of study—discovering the general reasons why students leave an institution—either longitudinal or synthetic models provide a structure for assessing the differential effects of several types of variables on the dropout decision. For the second type of study—predicting who will drop out—the "intent to leave" variable from the synthetic model has the highest correlation with actual attrition and is therefore most useful in identifying the potential dropout before the student leaves school. To evaluate the effectiveness of programs and services designed to reduce attrition, the synthetic model provides an appropriate means. The institutional researcher would need to introduce variables related to the extent and type of contact with the service or program under the category of "objective interaction with the organization." The relative influence of these variables on attrition can be assessed without loss of statistical control over other factors that affect attrition. For the final type of study—identifying the entry-level characteristics of the student who is most likely to stay in or to leave the institution—either the longitudinal-process or synthetic models would be suitable. Both allow for the introduction of variables that may affect the overall rates of attrition at an institution (for example, which students are admitted). This type of study may be of increased interest as institutions face the issue of what will happen to attrition rates if more inclusive criteria for admission are set.

None of the models presented here is completely satisfactory, and none can be used consistently to explain the majority of the variance in attrition

32

rates. Although the synthetic model orders certain relationships and uses the "intent to leave" variable to increase the explained variance substantially, the order of some of the variables (for example, absenteeism and grades) is not beyond debate, and saying that students leave because they intend to leave is not very useful for reducing or understanding student attrition. New models with new relationships will undoubtedly emerge in the next decade, and, with increased research, the number of variables in the current, complex models may well be reduced. Student attrition is an extremely complex process. Some of the causes may be identified and better understood, but there is no panacea.

References

Ajzen, I., and Fishbein, M. *Understanding Attitudes and Predicting Social Behavior.* Englewood Cliffs, N. J.: Prentice-Hall, 1980.

Bean, J. P. "Dropouts and Turnover: The Synthesis of a Causal Model of Student Attrition." Unpublished doctoral dissertation, University of Iowa, 1978.

Bean, J. P. "Path Analysis: The Development of a Suitable Methodology for the Study of Student Attrition." Paper presented at the annual meeting of the American Educational Research Association, San Francisco, April 1979.

Bean, J. P. "Dropouts and Turnover: The Synthesis and Test of a Causal Model of Student Attrition." *Research in Higher Education,* 1980, *12,* 155–187.

Bean, J. P. "Student Attrition, Intentions, and Confidence: Interaction Effects in a Path Model ($R^2 = .51$)." Paper presented at the annual meeting of the American Research Association, Los Angeles, April 1981.

Bean, J. P. "The Application of a Model of Turnover in Work Organizations to the Student Attrition Process." *Review of Higher Education* (in press).

Bentler, P. M., and Speckart, G. "Models of Attitude-Behavior Relations." *Psychological Review,* 1979, *86* (452), p. 464.

Biddle, B. J., and Thomas, E. J. (Eds.). *Role Theory.* New York: Wiley, 1966.

Durkheim, E. *Suicide.* Translated by J. Spaulding and C. Simpson. Glencoe, Ill.: The Free Press, 1961.

Fishbein, M., and Ajzen, I. *Belief, Attitude, Intention and Behavior: An Introduction to Theory and Research.* Reading, Mass.: Addison-Wesley, 1975.

Johnson, R. H. "The Relationship of Academic and Social Integration to Student Attrition—A Study Across Institutions and Institutional Types." Unpublished doctoral dissertation. Ann Arbor: The University of Michigan, 1980.

Kerlinger, F. L. *Foundations of Behavioral Research.* (2nd ed.). New York: Holt, Rinehart and Winston, 1973.

Lenning, O. T., Beal, P. E. and Sauer, K. *Retention and Attrition: Evidence for Action and Research.* Boulder, Colo. National Center for Higher Education Management Systems, 1980.

Locke, E. A. "The Nature and Causes of Job Satisfaction." In M. D. Dunnette (Ed.), *Handbook of Industrial and Organizational Psychology.* Chicago: Rand McNally, 1976.

Merton, R. K. *Social Theory and Social Process.* New York: Free Press, 1968.

Pascarella, E. "Student–Faculty Informal Contact and College Outcomes." *Review of Educational Research,* 1980, *50* 545–595.

Price, J. L. *The Study of Turnover.* Ames, Iowa: Iowa State University Press, 1977.

Price, J. L. and Mueller, C. W. "A Causal Model of Turnover for Nurses." *Academy of Management Journal,* 1981, *24,* 543–565.

Rootman, I. "Voluntary Withdrawal from a Total Adult Socialization Organization: A Model." *Sociology of Education,* 1972, *45,* 258–270.

Spady, W. "Dropouts from Higher Education: An Interdisciplinary Review and Synthesis." *Interchange,* 1970, *1,* 64–85.

Spady, W. "Dropouts from Higher Education: Toward an Empirical Model." *Interchange,* 1971, *2,* 38–62.

Tinto, V. "Dropout from Higher Education: A Theoretical Synthesis of Recent Research." *Review of Educational Research,* 1975, *45,* 89–125.

Thorngate, W. "In General versus It Depends: Some Comments on the Gergen-Schlenker Debate." *Personality and Social Psychology Bulletin,* 1976, *2,* 404–410.

John P. Bean is currently an assistant professor of higher education at Indiana University–Bloomington. Prior to this, he coordinated academic program reviews and evaluations and worked in the Office of Institutional Research and Planning at the University of Nebraska–Lincoln. His research has focused on the development and estimation of causal models of student attrition.

*Those studying persistence/attrition behavior need to give
considerable thought not only to the process by which variables
are selected but also to the adequacy with which they are measured.*

Variable-Selection and
Measurement Concerns

Oscar T. Lenning

Literally thousands of studies of student attrition have been conducted at
colleges and universities over the years, and invariably they have focused on
identifying student characteristics and other factors related to attrition, as well
as on causes of attrition. Understanding attrition and retention can help us
ascertain ways to improve the situation, and prediction studies may allow us to
identify dropout-prone students before it is too late to help them. Another type
of retention/attrition study has only recently received much attention — studies
of the effectiveness of various efforts to improve student retention. In all these
types of studies, some variables hold more promise than others for studying
attrition, and this will a major topic of discussion in this chapter. Another
focus of this chapter will be on data gathering and measurement concerns.

Variable Selection Consideration

In selecting variables for study and making measurement plans, we
need to consider a variety of factors, some inherent to the study and some
extraneous. After discussion of the universe of variables potentially appropriate for different kinds of attrition studies, such factors will be discussed.

Possible Independent/Predictor Variables for Attrition Studies. Many
student and institutional factors have potential relationships with college withdrawal, but the relationships are often complicated and not constant across in-

E. Pascarella (Ed.). *New Directions for Institutional Research: Studying Student Attrition*, no. 36.
San Francisco: Jossey-Bass, December 1982.

dividuals and groups. Many variables themselves are not worthy of study, but consideration should be given to controlling for them through subgrouping or other means. Some of the most promising independent variables refer neither to students nor to institutions, but are, rather, interaction variables (student-institution interactions). The summary that follows is based on the research syntheses of Cope and Hannah (1975), Lenning, Beal, and Sauer (1980), Lenning, Sauer, and Beal (1980), Pantages and Creedon (1978), and Ramist (1981).

Student Demographic Variables. These variables are usually not useful for predicting attrition, but certain subgroups tend to have larger percentages of dropouts and therefore deserve special attention. Separate predictions within such groups may be warranted.

Age. Older students tend to be "rusty" on academic skills, less able to adapt quickly to changing conditions, and slower in their work and thinking. These weaknesses are compensated by tendencies to be more highly motivated, more mature, and more traditional in their values. Therefore, results of different studies have often conflicted. How old students are, as well as their reason for attending college, programs taken, and status (for example, retired persons wanting enrichment, middle-aged retrainees, homemakers wanting to enter careers after raising their children), may be deciding factors. "Older" is not a very discriminating term, but age does seem to be related to reasons given for dropping out.

Sex. Sex differences in attrition can be accounted for largely by differences in motivation, socioeconomic level, marital status, and so forth. More men drop out during the freshman year and "stop out" more in terms of eventual dropout and transfers. Women are more likely to drop out when the male–female ratio is large; men are more likely to drop out at large nonselective universities. Men most often give academic reasons for dropping out, while women more often give nonacademic reasons.

Socioeconomic Status. Students from the lowest socioeconomic levels drop out more often than do more advantaged students. This is less the result of the parents' income and occupation than of their educational level. The educational level of parents is often related to how much they value a college education for their children, as well as to the type of environment they provided for students while they were growing up.

Ethnic Background. Hispanic students tend to drop out more often, irrespective of controls used; Asian and Jewish students, less often. Blacks and American Indians drop out more often, but such differences disappear when socioeconomic level, ability test scores, and motivation are controlled.

Marital Status. Marrying tends to increase men's chances and to decrease women's chances of persisting until graduation.

Hometown Location and Size. Students from rural areas have been found to drop out more often, but size and nature of the college may make a difference in whether this finding is valid. There have also been some data suggesting that out-of-state students from noncontiguous states drop out more often.

Student Academic Factors. These factors are important for predicting academic dismissals. They also often have an effect in cases of voluntary withdrawal.

Aptitude Test Scores. Lower college-admissions test scores and reading-test scores (such as on the Nelson-Denny) are related to higher attrition and imply that students have to work much harder to succeed in college. Reading ability is also related to other communication abilities important for college achievement (for example, the ability to write and speak effectively).

High School Achievement. High school grade point average and rank in high school class have been found to have a higher relationship to student attrition than any other single predictor. Even so, they account for only a small percentage of the variance, often less than 10 percent.

Study Habits and Attitudes. Students with poor study habits and attitudes tend to drop out more often.

High School Attended. Student ratings of the academic quality of the high school attended have been found to be directly related to student retention.

Subjects and Number of Courses Taken in High School. Those who took a college-preparatory program—and, within such a program, those who took more courses in English, mathematics, foreign languages, and physical sciences—tend to persist more. The number of courses in social studies and biological sciences has not been found to have such a relationship.

College Program. Students majoring in certain programs tend to drop out more often, while those in other programs tend to persist more often. These findings, however, vary by institution.

College Grades. Most of those who drop out of college have satisfactory grades, but dropouts do tend to have somewhat lower grades than persisters. Therefore, those who exhibit any sign of academic difficulty (for example, low grades, self-report of study problems) during the first term probably deserve special observation and attention.

Initial Student Aspirations and Motivational Variables. Ramist (1981) makes some noteworthy comments regarding motivational factors: "Student motivational factors may be considered the sine qua non of persistence, and therefore the most important target of persistence research. However, they may be considered so obviously related to persistence as to make research on the relationship trivial. With the exception of those who do not have the requisite ability, students continue in college because they choose to do so and drop out because they choose to do so, for reasons that may or may not be accurately assessed. For a student with the requisite ability, even involuntary withdrawal due to low grades is really voluntary: a result of the student's choice not to do the work that is necessary to obtain sufficiently high grades" (p. 10). As suggested by Ramist, determining the underlying reasons for the presence or absence of motivation to persist is the crucial research question for implementing a strategy to improve student retention. These reasons, however, are usually very complex and difficult to assess. Still, in early warning and prediction of attrition, strictly motivational factors (such as first-term GPA differences with ability controlled) are potentially crucial variables.

Degree Aspiration. Students aspiring to doctoral or professional degrees are more likely to persist than those with lower degree aspirations.

Termination/Completion Plans. Intention upon entrance to drop out (for example, students' expectations that they will dislike college and leave) suggests more likelihood of withdrawal, while a firm and concrete intention to persist suggests less likelihood to withdraw. Of course, these may be simply self-fulfilling prophecies, but if the expectation to succeed is unrealistic (or if the commitment to graduation is a compulsion symbolic of psychological stress), frustration, dissatisfaction, and disappointment leading to escapism can be the result.

Commitment to the College. Positively related to persistence, commitment to the college is absolutely necessary if persistence is to take place when there is not a good fit between the college and the student.

Vocational and Occupational Goals. This variable seems to be positively related to persistence for students in technological and vocational programs, but not in other programs.

Familial Aspirations for College. Strong parental aspirations or expectations for the student to attend and complete college relate positively to student retention, but Pantages and Creedon (1978) argue persuasively that this will hold true primarily when there is a quality relationship between parents and child or when conforming to parents' wishes is an inner pressure and ingrained lifestyle for the student. Dropping out is one way students can assert their independence from their parents.

Student Personality and Value Variables. Inconsistent findings have been reported for variables of this type, indicating complex relationships. Some of these findings, however, may be important when considered in relationship to the institutional environment.

Maturity and Responsibility. Those who are more mature, responsible, and clear in their goals and aspirations (when those goals need a college degree) will tend to persist. The exception may be in liberal arts, where there may be no attempt to show practical relationships between learning and vocational or other life after college.

Independence and Autonomy. When students show extreme orientation to independence and autonomy, a conformist college and classroom atmosphere will tend to result in withdrawal. Where the environment is more independence-oriented and student orientation to autonomy is not so extreme, the tendency is to persist.

Intellectual Orientation. Where the college environment is intellectual, the intellectual student will tend to persist; where the emphasis seems to be only on grades, some students may leave in disgust.

Creativity. William Faulkner, John Steinbeck, and Eugene O'Neill dropped out of college because the conformist environment was stifling their creativity and boring them. If the college environment does not support creativity, extremely creative people will tend to withdraw, unless other factors compensate or intervene.

Self-Concept. A positive self-concept and self-confidence will tend to lead students to persist, unless the concept of self and the college environment are in conflict.

Anxiety. Anxiety about success can lead to persistence, unless the anxiety becomes too great, at which point it becomes destructive and tends to lead to withdrawal.

Assertiveness. Assertiveness tends to be related to persistence except where it is ridiculed because others at the college see the assertive person as rude. A similar interaction obtains for creativity.

Value Orientation. How the student's value orientation and philosophy of life compare to the institutional value orientation will determine any relationship to student attrition.

Student Concern About Finances. Although lack of finances is often a real problem that discourages persistence and is the reason students most often give for dropping out, there is evidence that in many cases it is a problem more perceptual than real. Even when there is adequate financial support, either through the provision of work and financial aid or the family's ability to pay, finances are thought to be a socially acceptable reason for withdrawal, one that will protect the ego from having to divulge another, more immediate reason. Conversely, arrangements with even very limited financial resources are worked out by some students who have a strong commitment to persist, no matter what.

Expressed Need for Counseling. Those students at nonselective colleges who express a need for personal counseling tend to drop out more often than other students.

Institutional Variables. Institutional characteristics could also logically be expected to influence student attrition rates. Institutional variables that have had some support in research are listed below.

Prestige. Graduation rates tend to be higher at prestigious institutions.

Size. We can expect to see less student involvement at large institutions, a factor that could adversely affect student retention; a number of studies have found such a relationship. Other studies have found equal or better retention at large institutions, which suggests that variables other than size are the underlying causal factors.

Control. Privately controlled colleges tend to have higher student retention than public colleges.

Type. Four-year colleges tend to have higher retention than two-year colleges. Single-sex colleges generally have higher retention rates than coeducational institutions, but for males, student and other institutional variables seem to account for the difference.

Affiliation. Religious affiliation tends to mean higher student retention, and Catholic colleges tend to have higher retention rates than protestant colleges.

Selectivity. The more highly selective colleges tend to have higher student retention rates. This may be largely explained by the fact that they attract higher-ability students to begin with. Moreover, since they also tend to have higher prestige and costs, the financial and ego damage related to dropping out may be prohibitive.

Housing. Residential campuses tend to have higher retention rates than commuter campuses, and on-campus life in sororities and fraternities tends to promote student retention more than dormitory life does.

Student Services. The availability, quality, and use of student services such as counseling, advising, orientation, and learning centers tends to promote student retention.

Institutional Mission. Institutions that communicate a specific and clearly defined mission generally have higher retention rates.

Interaction Variables. Relationships of some student variables to student retention were said to vary with college characteristics. Thus, for example, students from rural areas tend to persist better at small, rural-oriented colleges than at large, metropolitan colleges. This is an example of an interaction variable; a number of interaction variables have been found to assist in the prediction of student attrition and retention.

Student Satisfaction. Satisfaction contributes to student persistence; dissatisfaction contributes to attrition only to the extent that attrition is not moderated by willingness to endure dissatisfaction.

Social Integration/Peer Group Relations. The frequency and quality of interaction with the peer group, as well as the kind and compatibility of student-peer group lifestyles and values, all affect student retention and persistence.

Family–College Relationship. The amount of commitment that the parents (and often the students) have to the college is related to student persistence.

Out-of-Class Interactions with Faculty. The frequency and especially the quality of student–faculty out-of-class interactions can often contribute substantially to student persistence.

Faculty Concern for Students and Teaching. The genuineness and strength of faculty members' interest in and concern for students and for helping them learn relates positively to student persistence.

Institutionally Generated Student Development. The amount of academic and intellectual development and other kinds of student growth and development tend to be positively associated with student persistence.

Commitment to the College and Graduation. Commitment to the college and to graduation is positively related to student persistence.

Extracurricular Involvement. Except when it is overdone, student involvement in extracurricular activities of various kinds, including campus employment, tends to support student persistence.

Responsiveness to Student Complaints and Expressed Needs. How well institutional personnel respond to student complaints and stated needs is a determinant of student persistence.

Student Expectations and Realities. The degree of congruence or discrepancy between what the student expects from the college and the reality of the college environment may be a major factor in persistence/withdrawal behavior.

Academic Program Involvement and Success. Quality involvement in honors programs or in foreign study programs, tutoring or peer counseling, instructional assisting, academic program review, or other involvement in the academic life of the college all contribute to student persistence.

Learning-Preferences and Teaching-Method Congruence. Research has demonstrated that learning styles vary from person to person; certain teaching styles and methods work best for students with particular learning styles. For example, conforming students learn better when there is structured teaching, and independence-oriented students learn better in an open, nonstructured classroom situation. Matches or mismatches in learning and teaching styles may influence persistence.

Compatibility Between Student and Institutional Values. When student attitudes, values, and lifestyle are congruent with those expressed by the college, student development and persistence are facilitated.

Student–Body Characteristics. When the student is similar to a significant group of other students at the college on factors such as town size, religion, and race, student persistence is enhanced.

Student Participation in Student Services. Student need for and participation in student services such as effective orientation, advising, counseling, and learning assistance positively affect persistence.

Student Ability and College Demands. As Pantages and Creedon (1978) noted, "The extent to which the student can meet the demands of the college and derive satisfaction from doing so is the degree to which the student may be expected to persist at the college" (p. 94).

Student and Comfortable Environment. Persistence should be positively influenced when the environment makes students comfortable (not unduly under stress and anxiety) but still challenges them to develop intellectually and personally.

Selecting Variables from this Universe. This extensive list of variables provides a universe from which institutional researchers can choose in planning research studies. It includes the major factors that retention research and theory suggest may directly or indirectly affect student persistence or attrition in particular contexts and situations. Other potentially useful variables found in student-achievement research could be added, including some of the additional variables discussed by Lenning and others (1974a, 1974b) in their work on nonintellective correlates of "college success." For example, they refer to a study of Benson (1967), which found that student reports of "marginal time utilization choices" were more significant to grade prediction than GPA or SAT scores.

We must consider a number of factors in selecting variables for student retention/attrition studies. The variables appropriate for one study may not be appropriate for another, while the same variable may be used as a predictor in one study, a moderator variable in a second study, or a subgrouping variable in a third.

Retention/Attrition Type

The dependent (criterion) variable of retention/attrition can refer to a number of different variables, each an appropriate phenomenon for study. Traditionally, "retention" has referred to completing a program at the institution entered in the time for which the program was designed (goal achievement), and "attrition" has meant not graduating in that length of time. The use of such a variable is not very meaningful at a community college, however, because of the stopping-in, stopping-out, and part-time enrollment that typifies student behavior at such colleges. Furthermore, if a student's goal is to obtain a secure job and he or she is offered such a position halfway through the program and accepts it, has the student really dropped out? If a student drops out in the middle of a course or a term, it may very well mean something different from dropout between terms; the cause of dropout often appears to vary with the point in the course or the term at which dropout occurs (beginning, middle, or end). Similarly, research suggests that different causal variables are often operating when a junior or a senior drops out, as compared to when a freshman drops out.

Lenning, Beal, and Sauer (1980) have identified some different types of student retention that call for different independent (predictor) variables and in certain cases call for differences in how such variables are examined or used for control purposes. The three basic categories of retention set forth are graduation, course or term completion, and personal goal attainment (when the goal is other than graduation). In each of these cases, retention implies attainment of the goal, and attrition implies lack of attainment.

There are subtypes within each category. For example, thinking in terms of the dimensions of time, institution, and program gives six basic subtypes of retention as graduation (Lenning, Sauer, and Beal, 1980): (1) graduating in the time designated for the degree or certificate offered, (2) graduating after the time designated for the degree or certificate offered, (3) graduating from an institution of initial entry, (4) graduating from an institution other than the one of initial enrollment, (5) graduating from the curricular program initially entered, and (6) graduating from a curricular program other than the one initially entered. As an example of how such differentiations affect data collection, the Student Attrition Task Force of the Council for the Advancement of Small Colleges (1978) recommended that a college determine attrition percentages by class and by year and that normative attrition percentages be available for small private colleges by college type (single-sex versus coeducational colleges), racial predominance, size, and region of the country. Many combinations of the six basic subtypes are possible, and a profile of institutional or program retention percentages for a selection of these subtype combinations could be useful to institutional or program staff in judging what is happening.

Other typologies of retention/attrition should also be mentioned when the different retention or attrition types imply that different variables are needed. Involuntary/discretionary dropouts will likely have some factors associated with them that are different from those of voluntary/nondiscretionary dropouts (a common differentiation). Other differentiations that imply varying factor relationships include satisfied dropouts/persisters versus dissatisfied dropouts/persisters and committed dropouts/persisters versus uncommitted dropouts/persisters.

Purpose of the Study

An attrition/retention study may be conducted for a number of different purposes, including (1) to determine retention rates that can serve as baselines for monitoring the effects of subsequent institutional or program changes; (2) to determine the causes of retention/attrition; (3) to identify correlates of retention; (4) to develop an early-warning prediction system to identify students who are potential dropouts; (5) to increase understanding of the withdrawal process; (6) to identify those students who will survive only if special support is provided and to determine what support is needed (those who will drop out no matter what the college does are of no concern here); (7) to ascertain students' reported reasons for dropping out (which research suggests are often different from the underlying, real reasons); (8) to show dropouts the college's concern for them (for example, exit interviews have been found to help change the minds of some students who are in the process of dropping out); (9) to assess the probable costs versus benefits of different retention program strategies; and (10) to evaluate special retention-program efficiency and/or effectiveness.

Such diverse purposes suggest that many variables will be involved in different ways. For example, the relationships between sex and retention/attrition summarized earlier suggest that a study to determine retention baseline percentages or to determine causes should use sex as a subgrouping variable; but sex would not be a good predictor variable in an early-warning prediction study. Similarly, the summary suggests that interaction variables may be the best candidates for predictors in an early-warning system, and some prediction study results confirm that such variables can be good predictors. For example, studies at Syracuse University (Pascarella and Terenzini, 1980) and at the State University of New York at Albany (Terenzini, Lorang, and Pascarella, 1980) used a thirty-four–item questionnaire with five interaction-variable scales that predicted 75 percent of the persisters and dropouts correctly. The five interaction-variables were peer group relations, informal interactions with the faculty, faculty's concern for student development and teaching, academic and intellectual development, and institutional/goal commitments. Control variables used in these studies were sex, race, liberal arts/professional program, ability test score, high school rank, parents' income, father's education, mother's education, degree expectation, whether the university was a first or a lower choice, freshman year GPA, freshman or high school extracurricular involvement, expected frequency of contact with faculty members, level of commitment to graduating, and preregistration confidence that this university was the right choice.

An earlier study of California community colleges (McMillan and Kester, 1973) found that the following variables (only some of which were interaction variables) contributed to the 68 percent classification accuracy yielded: ability, degree aspirations, perceived importance of college, parents' stress on college attendance, financial and employment concerns, family income, and race. In still another study, Blanchfield (1971) obtained 70 percent classification accuracy using (among others) the variables of Social Consciousness Test results, percentage of college expenses covered by grants, and high school rank.

Institutional Types and Characteristics

As shown in Table 1, excerpted from Beal and Noel's (1980) national survey, retention rates vary from one type of postsecondary institution to another. Within an institution, retention rates vary by program, and there is evidence that different situational and institutional factors are operating not only from one institution to another but also from one program to another within an institution. In addition to the purpose of the investigation, the research and theory related to salient institutional characteristics and situations present on campus (Lenning, Beal and Sauer, 1980) will suggest variables to be considered in planning the study. Once a list of tentative variables has been developed, the list can be refined and shortened through in-depth analysis of how the relevant research for this type of college and theory might apply in this case and through a small-scale, preliminary pilot test of the study, using only a few students of each type under consideration.

Construct Conciseness and Ease/Accuracy of Measurement

Unless one knows what a construct label implies, it is not very helpful for practical research done on campus, although the construct may still be heuristically very useful in stimulating and clarifying types of research and theory. The meaning of the results in terms of policy is often unclear; in certain study designs, the construct can contaminate results found for more straightforward and clear-cut variables. Furthermore, such imprecise constructs cannot be measured with reliability and precision. This is not to say that qualitative variables should not be used; qualitative factors may very well be the most crucial correlates of retention and attrition, and such factors can generally be tapped with some accuracy by a cluster of relatively concrete variables. In selecting those variables, available data-collection resources should be considered. When considered in concert, several easily collected measures may provide comparable accuracy to an accurate and reliable but costly or difficult measure of that factor.

Table 1. 1978 Graduation and Freshman Retention Rates for Undergraduate Programs by Institutional Type and Selectivity

	N^a	Graduation Rate[b]	N^c	Freshman Retention Rate
Two-Year Public Institutions				
Open Admissions	206	42%	105	54%
Liberal Admissions	7	55%	5	64%
Two-Year Private Institutions				
Open Admissions	14	54%	14	60%
Liberal Admissions	31	64%	16	63%
Traditional Admissions	3	65%	1	95%
Four-Year Public Institutions				
Open Admissions	41	46%	24	60%
Liberal Admissions	58	56%	55	66%
Traditional Admissions	26	55%	16	64%
Selective Admissions	19	59%	18	76%
Highly Selective Admissions	4	64%	2	80%
Four-Year Private Institutions				
Open Admissions	17	52%	18	52%
Liberal Admissions	153	57%	116	65%
Traditional Admissions	71	59%	47	71%
Selective Admissions	67	65%	50	79%
Highly Selective Admissions	19	77%	15	90%

[a]The numbers of each type providing graduation rate percentages as indicated in Footnote c below, and upon which the listed graduation percentages are based.

[b]For four-year institutions this is the percentage of 1973 entering freshman who had graduated at this college by the Spring of 1978, five years after entrance. For two-year institutions, this is the percentage of 1975 entering freshmen who had graduated with a degree or certificate by the spring of 1978, three years after entrance.

[c]The numbers of institutions of each type reporting end-of-freshman year retention percentages for 1977–78 freshmen, and upon which the listed freshman retention percentages are based.

Source: Beal and Noel, 1980.

We should not shrink from attempting to measure and use difficult-to-assess variables if research and theory suggest that such variables are important for understanding student retention. As Hoyt (1978, p. 78) stated, "A small number of studies have addressed the problem of matching student and college characteristics. These studies, too, have been largely unproductive, in part because we lack defensible taxonomies to guide our choice of characteristics. Are the most meaningful variables the ones that can be most easily addressed (size, affluence, type of control, location, complexity, selectivity)? Or would difficult-to-assess variables like faculty commitment to teaching, concern for personal values, vocational emphasis, or academic standards be more valuable? In addition, it is not altogether clear what is to be matched—the student with other students in the living group, with students in general, with students in the same curriculum, or with faculty members?"

Significance and Meaningfulness of the
Student–Institutional Relationship

Hoyt (1978) emphasizes the importance of understanding relationships with retention and the complexity of such relationships but syntheses of the various relevant theories by Bean (Chapter Two, this volume) and by Lenning, Beal, and Sauer (1980) make it clear that the key to understanding is a congruence between complex arrays of student and environmental factors and the dynamic interactions among them. Part of the picture is Feldman and Newcomb's (1969) explanation that adequate congruence between the perceived and actual demands, rewards, and constraints of the particular institutional settings (in terms of peers, instructors, policies and regulations, parental expectations, living conditions, interpersonal relations, and so forth) and the perceived and actual desires, goals, needs, interests, talents, and abilities of the student will positively influence retention. Thus interactions among variables within these institutional and personal areas should be a focus of study in terms of their associations with persistence/withdrawal behavior.

Hoyt's (1978) theoretical formulation is another part of the picture. He states the following:

> Persisting in college represents a choice that is available to most students. . . . Persistence will be chosen when satisfactions (both realized and anticipated) associated with it exceed those associated with any choice. . . . Lacking satisfaction in a given situation, individuals will "experiment" with alternative choices and select one that is judged to have the highest probablity of providing satisfaction. . . . Satisfactions arise from two sources: a sense of progress (including expected progress) in reaching personal goals and a sense of comfort with the environment (acceptance, security, freedom from pressure). . . . Enduring satisfactions (sound choices) require support from both sources of satisfaction. . . . The process of finding satisfaction is threatened by barriers that, in theory, can be removed. [Thus] attrition/retention research should begin with the collection of information about the student prior to enrollment. While traditional measures of academic potential should be included, it is perhaps more important to learn about such other characteristics as goals and aspirations (clarity, commitment to a given plan), institutional attractiveness, and potential barriers to program completion (finances, health, incompatible but competing desires, educational deficiencies). . . . It is especially important to learn about "process variables" which affect satisfaction, directly or indirectly. For example, experiences related to interpersonal contacts (making friends, dating, sharing ideas), faculty contacts (experiences that convey the impression that a faculty member is aware of and sensitive to the student as an individual), situational investment (joining clubs or organized groups, becoming a "member" of anything identified with the

institution), reinforcements/punishments (feedback that makes the individual feel successful or rewarded, discouraged, or humiliated), experiences related to overcoming barriers (solidifying financial situation, improving reading skills), and experiences aimed at self-understanding (counseling, exploratory or try-out experiences, formal appraisals) [pp. 79–82].

In addition, Hoyt states that satisfaction should be assessed in terms of perceived opportunity relevance, commitment, perceived comfort and sense of well-being in the environment, and perceived personal progress in the cognitive (for example, grades received), affective, and motor areas. All these measures should be collected periodically over the student's career, so that satisfied and dissatisfied persisters and dropouts who are committed and uncommitted (six groups) can be compared and attrition patterns better understood. Tinto's (1975) model emphasizes that *commitment* means commitment both to graduation and to the institution (both commitments are important to persistence and depend on personal characteristics and background experiences), and that satisfaction depends on both academic integration and social integration.

Other parts of the picture include orientation of the person versus orientation of the environment, for example, Holland's (1963, 1973) realistic, intellectual, social, conventional, enterprising and artistic categories of personality and environment; expectations of the environment versus what is later found to be reality; personal values and lifestyle versus campus values and lifestyle; student tolerance for ambiguity versus amount of ambiguity present in the environment; student ability to put up with dissatisfaction versus amount of dissatisfaction present; student learning styles versus instructional styles; presence or absence of "significant others"; expectations of success versus attained success; perceptions of self in relation to the institution; and involvement in the environment. Which of these many variables to consider and how to use them depends so much on institutional context and the purpose of the research that no overall generalization can be made here. Logic, in-depth knowledge, and understanding of the particular context and situation must guide such decision making.

Other Considerations in Selecting Variables

Tabulating reported student reasons for dropping out has probably been the most common type of attrition study. There is evidence, however (Demitroff, 1975; Demos, 1968), that the felt need by dropouts to have their responses be socially acceptable (and in various areas it may be an unconscious effort to protect egos) biases the results. Thus, where possible, confirming evidence such as observations by trained counselors should also be collected and discrepancies noted. Dropouts' perceptions of why they drop out should not be ignored, however; dropout rationales, even if they are rationalized, stimulate and guide action, but since we basically know what most dropouts will say, little special time and effort should be devoted to planning such self-report studies. What is needed is a routinized exit-interview system.

The usefulness of particular variables found at similar institutions should also be considered in selecting variables and deciding how to apply them. The experiences of others, however, must be analyzed carefully in terms of how your students and your institution differ.

Measurement Concerns and Considerations

Several factors related to measurement in retention and attrition have already been stated or implied, because variables and measurement are closely intertwined. This section focuses specifically on measurement as it relates to such studies.

As stated previously, some variables are clear-cut and easy to measure, while others are qualitative and difficult to measure with validity and reliability. Thus "sex ratio," "student body ability level," and "institutional size" need one number each (or two at most) to represent them, while "campus-life orientation," "faculty commitment to teaching," and "quality of student–faculty interactions" are complex arrays that need several indices to provide some semblance of validity and reliability. As also suggested earlier, however, the more complex and multifaceted interaction variables definitely show the most promise of being salient factors in our understanding of student persistence/ withdrawal behavior; therefore, such variables should be selected and used, as appropriate, depending on the purpose of the study and other factors delineated earlier. Nevertheless, multiple measures (for example, observation, questionnaire, interview, secondary data, unobtrusive measures) and data sources for the same measure (for example, student self-perceptions, student peer perceptions, faculty and staff perceptions, critical incidents, relevant facts) may be needed if adequate validity and reliability are to be attained. Where one measure/data source of the variable is weak, another will possibly be strong. Furthermore, where all the measures for the variable of concern indicate the same status, or where discrepancies are understood and accounted for, there is some assurance that reality is being assessed. In general, a key to reliability, accuracy, and validity is to keep observation and report at a specific, concrete level. Once questions in a questionnaire or interview become vague, abstract, and broad, the meaning and usefulness of the information collected becomes threatened.

It is one thing to say you are going to use relevant multiple measures and sources of data in longitudinal studies; it is quite another to carry this intention out. The following factors are needed for developing a practical, useful study that will affect the campus positively: resourcefulness; ability to weigh costs versus benefits; creativity in measure/indicator development and application; in-depth knowledge of what the research literature indicates; familiarity with what has worked and not worked elsewhere and how it relates to one's own campus and situation and a firm, well-defined, theoretical framework to guide variable selection, data collection, and data analysis. It is important to keep the study from getting too complex, cumbersome, and costly. At the same time, however, it is important to realize that retention and attrition are complex phenomena and require studies with considerable conceptual and technical sophistication. Perhaps the approach that would meet both needs would involve limiting the scope of the particular study (for example, through focusing separately on specific student subpopulations); conducting better-designed, small-sample, limited-focus studies under one theoretical framework, rather than one large, multifaceted and multifocus study; and pilot testing each study with small "convenience" samples (piloting would also allow needed design modifications and refinements to be made before implementation of the main study).

The use of interviews should not be rejected out of hand because of projected effort, time, and monetary requirements (for example, if one were to go to alumni or to dropouts who have left). As mentioned previously, exit interviews have resulted in some direct monetary return on investment, in terms of the up to 10 percent of students who change their minds about dropping out after chatting with well-trained exit interviewers. Interviews provide the best anecdotal information (often found to be the most helpful in understanding and clarifying causes and effects) and can contribute greatly to our view of the total picture, but they must be carefully designed, controlled, and carried out, and the interviewers must be well trained.

Studies involving interviews do not have to be expensive. For example, Kegan (1978) reported an attrition study that had major positive impacts at Hampshire College and involved telephone and interviewer costs of less than $350. Through discovery that attrition was more serious than they had perceived and that student social isolation and the quality of student life were root problems, college administrators developed and implemented a special retention-improvement program.

A serious barrier to effective retention/attrition studies at many institutions is keeping track of students as they persist, drop out, or stop out. Before data can be collected, we must know specifically where to find data. If studies are to be of manageable size and complexity and at the same time longitudinal, we must be able to follow each cohort of entering students through the college career. Computerized tracking systems have been developed that are effective for such purposes—see for example, Erwin and Tollefson (1982), Newlon and Gaither (1980), and Tilton (1979).

In designing a data-collection plan, whether it be for a retention/attrition study or some other study, a number of specific steps are important:

- Determining what the study should attempt to accomplish
- Ascertaining the environmental factors that will assist or constrain the assessment effort and developing a plan to overcome the constraints
- Determining the specific questions the study should help answer
- Specifying the evidence required to answer the study questions

- Outlining strategies and procedures for gathering and analyzing data (including ensuring an adequate questionnaire-response rate) that are feasible from the point of view of time required, resources available, payoff expected, efficiency, and effectiveness
- Determining how the information might be interpreted and used
- Indicating how all the above steps fit together in an integrated study under a clear-cut, theoretical framework.

See Lenning (1980) for some helpful general discussion related to each of these steps. Some of the specific steps for retention studies are also discussed by Patrick, Myers, and VanDusen (1979), but only in a much more limited sense (the focus is entirely on using attrition questionnaires).

Special mention should be made of the second step (above) which applies to variable selection as well as to the development of measurement plans. I was a consultant recently on student retention for a state university where a task force on student retention had been formed three years earlier. The task force had been formed because freshman enrollment had suddenly decreased, causing the faculty and the administration to start worrying about the decrease in the traditional student population that had already been projected for the early 1980s. Since retention was low on this campus, improved retention was seen as a way to keep enrollment up. By 1980, however, when the task force had completed its study and recommended ways to improve the university's retention rate, the university had returned to its previous pattern of enrolling more students than it could handle adequately. With the previous enrollment pattern reasserting itself, the task force's recommendations fell on deaf ears, and little interest remained on the campus in working to improve student retention.

There was a core group of administrators and faculty members (including the task force) who remained very concerned about student retention, however, and they decided they needed a consultant to advise them on strategies for gaining renewed campus support. It seemed clear to me that continuing to emphasize retention would be useless. Since, however, there was a strong concern throughout the campus for an image of quality, the group was advised to consider the formation of a task force on "quality of student life." This change in focus from retention to quality would fit in with the current politics and program focus throughout the campus and, perhaps, accomplish the results that could not be accomplished under a program of student retention. The findings that prestigious individuals and groups (including top-level administration) on campus will accept as evidence of a retention problem and what should be done about it must be carefully considered as one decides on variables, measures, and data sources for a study. Such things as campus customs, practices, values, personalities, bureaucratic organization, and the political situation are factors crucial to study design and implementation. They can be either constraints or facilitating factors. Special care must be devoted to taking best advantage of facilitating factors and determining ways to overcome or get around constraining factors (or at least make them less detrimental).

Response bias is a special problem in questionnaires sent to students who have dropped out of college. Those who do not respond may be those who are most dissatisfied and want the college to leave them alone. Conversely, some who are really dissatisfied might want to get back at the college by completing the questionnaire in a misleading way. The choice of questionnaire items and their wording can also be biasing and confounding factors because of the feelings and emotions they can bring about in students who drop out. One cannot divorce response bias from variable, measure, and data-source selection.

Conclusion

It should be emphasized that no one study, especially an institutional study, could include even half of the variables listed in the first section of this chapter. The researcher is going to have to select carefully, based on his or her theory of retention, knowledge of the literature, knowledge of the local context and situation, and input from advisory committees.

Valid and reliable instruments and procedures are needed for collecting accurate, relevant, and useful data. In addition, validity and reliability can be improved greatly through the use of multiple measures and data sources for the same construct. This should be done whenever it is possible in terms of available time and other resources.

Retention/attrition researchers have generally paid attention to content and predictive validity, although they often have not attempted to control for confounding variables that give misleading predictive results. There has been serious inattention, however, to construct validity, that is, the selection and measurement of variables guided by theory. Most previous research has been descriptive and atheoretical. Therefore, there is often only a scant conceptual framework to guide researchers in selecting and measuring the variables that represent salient constructs. With recent retention theory emphasizing meaningful interactions between students and the college, however, as well as the exemplary research that has been used to test the theories of Holland (1966, 1973), Spady (1970, 1971), and Tinto (1975), this should change soon.

Almost all research thus far, whether institutional or on a large scale, has focused on graduation as the criterion of retention. Institutional attention to course/term completion and personal goal attainment is also badly needed; different variables and measures may be needed for some of this research. Greater attention to time of attrition and to whether it is voluntary or involuntary is also necessary.

Another shortcoming in the research until now has been the dearth of retention/attrition studies for special subgroups such as transfer students; minority groups—Astin's (1975) research makes clear that "minority group" is too broad a term, and that each racial/ethnic group should be examined separately; and adult groups (retirees, retrainees, homemakers preparing for careers after their children are grown, and so forth). Most colleges and universities do not even record separate retention rates for such groups, much less focus on them in explanatory, predictive studies.

This chapter has concentrated on institutional retention research. If the description of the institution and its context is clear, if there is good documentation, and if careful attention is given to the manner in which variables and measures are selected and the data collected, analyzed, and interpreted, the pattern of similarities or discrepancies across the results of many local studies can be revealing and useful for all colleges and universities. Such care will also make the single-institution study more useful locally.

References

Beal, P. E., and Noel, L. *What Works in Student Retention*. Iowa City, Iowa, and Boulder, Colo.: American College Testing Program and National Center for Higher Education Management Systems.

Benson, P. H. "Multiple-Regression Analysis of a Paired-Choice Division of Time Inventory in Relation to Grade Point Average." *Journal of Applied Psychology*, 1967, *51*, 82–88.

Blanchfield, W. C. "College Dropout Identification: A Case Study." *Journal of Experimental Education*, 1971, *40*, 1–4.

Cope, R., and Hannah, W. "Revolving College Doors: The Causes and Consequences of Dropping Out, Stopping Out, and Transferring." New York: Wiley, 1975.

Council for the Advancement of Small Colleges. *User's Manual for the Student Attrition Module*. Washington, D. C.: Council for the Advancement of Small Colleges, 1978.

Demitroff, J. F. "Student Persistence." *College and University*, 1974, *49*, 553–565.

Demos, G. D. "Analysis of College Dropouts: Some Manifest and Covert Reasons." *Personnel and Guidance Journal*, 1968, *46*, 681–684.

Erwin, T. D., and Tollefson, A. L. "A Data Base Management Model for Student Development." *Journal of College Student Personnel*, 1982, *23*, 70–76.

Feldman, K. A., and Newcomb, T. M. *The Impact of College on Students*. San Francisco: Jossey-Bass, 1969.

Holland, J. L. *The Psychology of Vocational Choice: A Theory of Personality Types and Model Environments*. Waltham, Mass.: Blaisdell, 1966.

Holland, J. L. *Making Vocational Choices: A Theory of Careers*. Englewood Cliffs, N. J.: Prentice-Hall, 1973.

Hoyt, D. P. "A Retrospective and Prospective Examination of Retention-Attrition Research." In L. Noel (Ed.), *New Directions for Student Services: Reducing the Dropout Rate*, no. 3. San Francisco: Jossey-Bass, 1978.

Kegan, D. L. "The Quality of Student Life and Financial Costs: The Cost of Social Isolation." *Journal of College Student Personnel*, 1978, *19*, 55–58.

Lenning, O. T. "Assessment and Evaluation." In U. Delworth and G. R. Hanson (Eds.), *Student Services: A Handbook for the Profession*. San Francisco: Jossey-Bass, 1980.

Lenning, O. T., Beal, P. E., and Sauer, K. *Retention and Attrition: Evidence for Action and Research*. Boulder, Colo.: National Center for Higher Education Management Systems, 1980.

Lenning, O. T., Sauer, K., and Beal, P. E. *Student Retention Strategies*. Washington, D.C.: American Association for Higher Education, 1980.

Lenning, O. T., Munday, L. A., Johnson, O. B., Vander Well, A. R., and Brue, E. J. *Nonintellective Correlates of Grades, Persistence, and Academic Learning in College*. ACT Monograph 14. Iowa City, Iowa: American College Testing Program, 1974a.

Lenning, O. T., Munday, L. A., Johnson, O. B., Vander Well, A. R., and Brue, E. J. *The Many Faces of College Success and Their Nonintellective Correlates*. ACT Monograph 15. Iowa City, Iowa: American College Teaching Program, 1974o.

McMillan, T., and Kester, D. "Promises to Keep: NORCAL Impact on Student Attrition. *Community and Junior College Journal*, 1973, *43*, 45-46.

Newlon, L. L., and Gaither, G. H. "Factors Contributing to Attrition: An Analysis of Program Impact on Persistence Patterns." *College and University*, 1980, *55*, 237-251.

Pantages, T. J., and Creedon, C. F. "Studies of College Attrition: 1950-1975." *Review of Educational Research*, 1978, *48*, 49-101.

Patrick, C., Myers, E., and VanDusen, W. *A Manual for Conducting Student Attrition Studies*. (Rev. Ed.) Boulder, Colo., and New York: National Center for Higher Education Management Systems and the College Board, 1979.

Pascarella, E. T., and Terenzini, P. T. "Predicting Freshman Persistance and Voluntary Dropout Decisions from a Theoretical Model." *Journal of Higher Education*, 1980, *51*, 60-75.

Ramist, L., *College Student Attrition and Retention*. College Board Report No. 81-1. New York: College Entrance Examination Board, 1981.

Spady, W. G. "Dropouts from Higher Education: An Interdisciplinary Review and Synthesis." *Interchange*, 1970, *1*, 64-85.

Spady, W. G. "Dropouts from Higher Education: Toward an Empirical Model." *Interchange*, 1971, *2*, 38-62.

Terenzini, P. T., Lorang, W. G., Jr., and Pascarella, E. T. "Predicting Freshman Persistence and Voluntary Dropout Decisions: A Replication." Paper presented at the annual convention of the American Educational Research Association, Boston, April 1980.

Tilton, B. D. "The Development and Use of a Computerized Data Base for Monitoring Student Retention." Paper presented at the annual forum of the Association for Institutional Research, San Diego, May 1979.

Tinto, V. "Dropout from Higher Education: A Theoretical Synthesis of Recent Research." *Review of Educational Research*, 1975, *45*, 89-125.

Oscar T. Lenning is vice president and academic dean at Roberts Wesleyan College, Rochester, New York. He was formerly on the staff at the National Center for Higher Education Management Systems and the American College Testing Program.

How does one collect good data?
How does one analyze it?

Designing Attrition Studies

Patrick T. Terenzini

Despite an extraordinarily large literature and several excellent reviews (see Cope and Hannah, 1975; Spady, 1970; Tinto, 1975; Pantages and Creedon, 1978), attrition studies continue to be common assignmen:s for institutional researchers. The reasons for the interest in the sources of attrition are not hard to discern: In a period when enrollment declines ranging from 20 to 35 percent are forecast, higher educational administrators recognize that retention of enrolled students may be more effective and less costly than locating and enrolling new or transfer students. Moreover, the time and energies of admissions officers, faculty members, financial aid officers, counselo:s, residence hall staffs, and other personnel are expended on those students who leave, as well as on those who earn degrees or otherwise accomplish their goals. The financial and psychic costs to students may never be accurately known.

The issue before administrators, however, is not really now to retain students but, rather, how to retain those who can meet the academic requirements, would like to continue, and would benefit from an education at the institution. What aspects of students' experience over which the institution has some control tend to promote retention or attrition? This is the question that administrators and institutional researchers must address; and, the number of excellent literature reviews notwithstanding, it is a question many institutions must seek to answer for themselves. Literature reviews provide a general and useful understanding of the complexity of the attrition phenomenon, but in no way do they substitute for the local research many institutional research offices

E. Pascarella (Ed.). *New Directions for Institutional Research: Studying Student Attrition,* no. 36.
San Francisco: Jossey-Bass, December 1982.

are asked to undertake. This chapter attempts to provide some ideas on how best to collect and analyze data on attrition.

General Considerations

The need for a clear definition of "attrition" is acute: The selection of a definition will shape virtually every design and methodological consideration that follows it — the data collection design, the variables selected, the sampling plan and sample size, and the analytical procedures. The time invested in a careful and complete specification of what attrition means will pay excellent dividends in the long run.

The time period involved is another design consideration. In some instances, retention from matriculation to graduation may be the focus of attention. In other cases, retention during the first two years may be central. For community colleges or programs designed to meet more short-range student needs or to provide specialized and focused education, program retention or retention over a semester or a year may be of greater concern. Studies of attrition over short periods make significantly fewer design and implementation demands than studies of withdrawal over longer periods.

Specification of the target population — the group of students among whom attrition/retention patterns are of interest — is a third important consideration. Do we wish to know something about sources of attrition/retention at the campus level? Within an entering cohort? Among transfer students? Among community college students? Different answers to these questions will require different approaches.

Finally, designing a study is to some extent a series of compromises, and if compromise is inevitable, then it behooves us to know what is being gained and given away and at what price. This chapter attempts to describe some of the more common compromises we must make in designing attrition studies. A theory will help us make wise choices.

The term "design" is used to refer to a planned set of procedures that will be followed to test a set of hypotheses or answer a series of questions. Designs are considered, here to be of two general types — those for collecting information and those for analyzing it.

Data-Collection Designs

Three basic data-collection designs will be considered: (1) the "autopsy," or post hoc design, (2) the cross-sectional design, and (3) the longitudinal design. Each has its own assets and liabilities and they are treated here in ascending order, according to their complexity and the strength of their claims to scientific rigor.

The "Autopsy" Design. "Autopsy," retrospective, or post hoc attrition-study designs involve identifying students who have withdrawn from the institution and then sending them survey questionnaires. The survey instrument might ask students about why they withdrew, how often they used certain academic and student services, and their evaluations of those services, or about other features of their college experiences (for example, academic advising, adequacy of living arrangements, and peer relations). Such questionnaires might also ask about students' current activities, plans for the future, and possible plans to return to the institution. Such surveys are also occasionally used to encourage dropouts to reenroll.

This design seems straightforward enough: If you want to know why students drop out, ask them. Despite its appeal to common sense, however, the liabilities of this approach probably outweigh its assets. Common sense, in this instance flies in the face of good research design.

As Campbell and Stanley (1962, p. 6) note, "Basic to scientific evidence... is the process of comparison, of recording differences, or of contrast.... Securing scientific evidence involves making at least one comparison." The concept of controlled comparison is, then fundamental to what is scientific about research design. More specifically, controlled comparisons provide for the internal validity of a study. "Internal validity" refers to the design's capability of ensuring that an observed relation between an independent and a dependent variable is not spurious and that alternative explanations for the observed relation have been controlled and can be ruled out. Basically, internal validity can be enhanced in either of two ways: (1) through the random assignment of persons to experimental and control groups (probably impossible in attrition studies) or (2) through the use of a nonequivalent comparison group with statistical controls (discussed below) to take initial group differences into account.

While no naturally occurring attrition design can use random assignment, of the designs discussed here, only the autopsy study design typically fails to provide for a comparison group of dropouts. Data can be collected from nondropouts, although this occurs rarely; such information is likely to be gathered at different times and under different conditions from those provided by dropouts. In the absence of a comparison group, we can only describe dropouts' characteristics, attitudes, or behaviors — traits that may or may not be different from those of nondropouts. Without a comparison group, of course, statistical controls are meaningless.

The autopsy design also tends to produce comparatively low response rates. It is not uncommon to receive responses from fewer than half the students who have dropped out. While such response rates are not inherently undesirable, they are generally accompanied by three other very unwelcome conditions — sample unrepresentativeness, a diminished likelihood of identifying reliable differences, and constraints on the choice of analytical procedures. Fenstemacher (1973), for example, found that unrepresentativeness in an autopsy study is likely with respect both to the personal characteristics of dropouts and to their evaluations of their college experiences (respondents are likely to be more positive than nonrespondents). It can be shown mathematically that, as sample size increases, the ability of statistical tests to detect reliable differences also increases. Moreover, multivariate analytical procedures (highly desirable and discussed below) require a ratio of five subjects for each variable, if stable results are to be produced. An even higher ratio (perhaps twenty to one) is desirable if we wish to derive a regression equation for predicting individual behavior.

Information collected by using an autopsy design probably also has limited use for planning or evaluation, other than for purposes associated with attrition. The limitations proceed from the absence of a comparison group of nondropouts, from the fact that most autopsy data are collected after students have withdrawn, and from the questionable validity of the responses obtained.

If the research assets of the autopsy design are meager, however, the planning and implementation costs are correspondingly minimal. The training and experience required to conduct such a study are modest compared with those needed for the other designs. The services of a full-time researcher are probably not required, although short-term consultation with someone familiar with statistics and survey research techniques probably would be useful. Furthermore, since only one data collection is normally involved, the time necessary to collect and analyze the data is relatively brief, probably no more than four or five months.

Direct costs such as postage, computing time, materials, and printing expenses are also relatively modest in comparison with other designs discussed here. The major cost will most likely be first-class postage. Do not try to save mony by using bulk mailing rates: Such mail is not forwardable and will not be returned if undeliverable. Bower and Myers (1976) offer an excellent description of survey procedures.

The Cross-Sectional Design. "Cross-sectional" refers to the one-time collection of data from currently enrolled students. It amounts to an informational snapshot of the students at a single moment in their college careers. If year-to-year attrition is the primary interest, data might be collected near the end of an academic year; at community colleges, it might be best to gather data at the end of both semesters of an academic year. At the start of the next academic year or semester, sample members who fall into the various categories of dropouts and nondropouts are identified, and the groups are then compared on the variables thought to influence attrition decisions.

While the autopsy design's principal (and fatal) weaknesses are failure to provide for a comparison group of nondropouts and inability to control precollege differences between students who drop out and those who do not, a comparison group of nondropouts is a major feature of the cross-sectional design. This approach permits comparison of dropouts and nondropouts on the same measures, taken at the same time and under similar conditions. In addition, this design involves the measurement of potentially attrition-related experiences and attitudes at the very time they are presumably exerting their influence (Pantages and Creedon, 1978).

Whether potentially confounding precollege differences between the study groups will seriously threaten the internal validity of the study depends on the measures selected for inclusion in the data set. This problem is inherent in ex post facto research (see Kerlinger, 1973, pp. 378–394), in that a phenomenon is investigated after it occurs, and no opportunity exists to ensure the precollege similarity of the various groups (recall that random assignment is not possible). Thus, if we simply gather cross-sectional data on a group of students, later distinguish the dropouts from the nondropouts, and then compare the groups on a number of variables, we may very well find that the two groups are different, but it may be that the groups were different even before they came to college. Perhaps one group was more "attrition-prone" than the other before they ever arrived on campus. Failure to control for those differences may lead the researcher (unwittingly and, perhaps, quite expensively) to conclude that the sources of attrition lie within the institution's control, when in fact they do not. Scarce resources may then be invested in retention programs that have little chance of success, since a symptom has been taken for a cause.

Students' admission files and other institutional records may contain some information useful for controlling precollege differences, but opportunities for using such controls are probably limited. Information relating to such potentially important attrition predictors as precollege commitment to completion of a degree, educational and career aspirations or goals, and expectations of the college experience probably will be unavailable. To the extent that such precollege differences (including high school achievement and academic aptitude) can be controlled, we can have increased confidence that attrition/retention decisions are influenced by features of the institutional experience, not by precollege differences in disguise. Moreover, because the students are surveyed while on campus, the likelihood of acceptable response rates is increased, relative to the autopsy design. As noted earlier, the higher the response rate, the greater the likelihood that real differences among groups will be detected. This should not be taken to mean that detectable differences are educationally or administratively important; the reference is to statistical significance only.

The analytical procedures brought to bear on cross-sectional data, like those used in evaluating autopsy information, are more a function of the researcher's training and experience that of the design selected. Nothing inherent in any of these basic designs requires or proscribes the use of either bivariate or multivariate statistical procedures. If the design includes plans to control initial group differences, however, multivariate statistical procedures will be needed. This topic is discussed below.

The training and experience required of persons doing cross-sectional studies can vary considerably. A cross-sectional plan without controls may be as simple and direct as an autopsy design, but if the strengths of the cross-sectional design are to be maximized (contrasting dropouts with nondropouts and controlling for basic precollege differences), the services of a reasonably experienced researcher will probably be needed.

While only one major data collection is needed from students, the cross-sectional plan may encompass the hiatus between academic years and thus may take somewhat longer to complete than an autopsy study; between six and nine months may be required. In community colleges, if attrition between semesters is of interest, less time will be needed.

Although the direct costs of adopting a cross-sectional design could be as low as those associated with an autopsy study, they will probably be somewhat higher. The additional costs are related most directly to the need for sampling nondropouts; the likelihood (but not necessity) of collecting more information from each respondent; and, if controls are to be applied, the increased clerical and machine costs associated with merging into a single file the survey data and the information from sources other than the respondents (for example, from admissions files).

The cross-sectional design, in providing for a comparison group of nondropouts can be aggregated in order to examine relations between or among selected student characteristics and other attitudes or behaviors. For example, one might compare minority and nonminority students; commuting and resident students; males and females; or students in different academic majors with respect to academic performance, general attitudes toward academic or nonacademic programs, and evaluations of policies and services. In brief, the data collected from an attrition study based on the cross-sectional design described here can serve a variety of program, planning, and evaluation purposes.

Finally, as we seek to control initial group differences, the amount of planning and the data-management problems will increase. Compared to those of a longitudinal design, however, such demands are still relatively slight.

Longitudinal Designs. If a cross-sectional design produces an informational snapshot of students at one moment in their college careers, then a longitudinal (or "panel") design represents something of a family album, involving the same information collected at two or more points in time. Under this design, data on characteristics, goals, commitment levels, expectations, and so on are collected from entering students, either prior to or at matriculation. Additional data are collected near the end of the academic year or semester from respondents to the original survey. This data set would be designed to describe students' first-year or first-semester experiences, their current attitudes, or personal changes that could influence a decision to continue enrollment or to withdraw. Depending on the questions under study, longitudinal studies may run for one year or for a number of years. At various points over the lifetime of the study, members of the original sample who have dropped out of school (or, perhaps, dropped out and returned) are compared with their nondropout peers on the variables for which information is available.

Institutions that participate in national precollege student information programs, such as the Cooperative Institutional Research Program (sponsored jointly by the American Council on Education and the University of California at Los Angeles) or the American College Testing Program's Assessment Program, have a decided advantage over institutions that do not participate. The precollege information those programs provide constitutes an excellent data base for longitudinal studies of attrition, as well as for a variety of other educational programs, processes, and outcomes. All that is required are suitable follow-up studies.

While the cross-sectional design offers a substantial improvement over the autopsy design through the addition of a comparison group of nondropouts and some statistical controls for precollege differences, the longitudinal design provides for the extensive planned control of many variables thought to be potential influences on the attendance behavior of students. For this reason, the longitudinal design is the most internally valid of the designs discussed. Information collected prior to matriculation can be used statistically to equate dropouts and nondropouts. In an ex post facto situation, such statistical leveling may be as close as we can hope to come to the group equivalence afforded by random assignment of persons to groups.

Longitudinal designs, like cross-sectional ones, are likely to produce adequately high response rates. Since data are initially collected prior to the start of college experience (or very soon after it begins), the design benefits from new students' generosity in providing information requested by the institution. The precollege and freshman year–end data collections show comparatively high response rates, but such cooperation does not last forever. Since subsequent data collections are made only from previous respondents, response rates (when based on the size of the original sample) will decline with each data collection. The problem is unique to this design, and it is absolutely essential to take this increasing subject mortality into account when selecting a sample size for the initial data collection. The original sample size must be large enough to ensure that the estimated response rates for each subsequent data collection will yield enough respondents with complete data in each analytical group to permit stable statistical analyses. The safest rule of thumb is to begin with the largest original sample the study can afford.

The cumulative respondent mortality in longitudinal designs has important implications for the representativeness of persons who respond to all data requests. Clearly, as the percentage of the original sample declines with each data collection, the prospects for maintaining respondent representativeness will also decline. The only solution to this problem is making every effort to obtain responses from all members of the original sample or, in subsequent data collections, from all persons who have responded to earlier requests. Methods exist to adjust for unrepresentativeness that may occur as respondent mortality increases, but adjustment is no substitute for high response rates.

As we have seen, however, each design exacts its price. The longitudinal approach may be the most sound methodologically, but it is also the most expensive. Its adoption will require at least one person with well-developed social-science research skills, including familiarity with sampling designs, instrument construction, data-set management, and multivariate statistical analysis. Longitudinal studies require substantially more time to complete than either cross-sectional or autopsy designs: A longitudinal study any shorter than one year is not likely to provide much useful information on attrition. The time lapse between study initiation and preliminary results in a freshman-to-sophomore–year attrition study can easily take fifteen months. Direct costs will also be higher for longitudinal studies; the higher price is associated with the need for larger samples, and these beget larger numbers of instruments, more mailings, increased coding volume, and more computer time.

Other planning considerations include the increased need for careful study design, instrument development, and sampling design. What would be minor oversights in an autopsy study can burgeon into major and costly problems in a longitudinal design. Depending on the availability of suitable computer software, the data-management problems involved in merging files of unequal sizes can be burdensome. File-merging operations that cannot be done by machine will have to be done manually, adding to the time and clerical assistance required.

Table 1 gives a summary evaluation of the three basic data-collection designs discussed. The following section describes a number of ways we can analyze the data collected.

Data-Analysis Designs

A substantial number (perhaps even the vast majority) of attrition studies rely on univariate or bivariate statistical procedures. In some instances, such studies employ little more than a series of frequency and percentage distributions. In other cases, the data analysis consists of repeated bivariate tests of significance (for example, Chi Square tests of association, t-tests, or one-way analyses of variance). Fortunately, such practices are waning as institutional researers become more familiar with multivariate statistical procedures and the packaged computer programs to perform them (for example, SPSS, BMD-P, and SAS).

Repeated bivariate tests of significance lead to several problems. First, as the number of such tests increases, the likelihood of obtaining a falsely significant result increases. For example, one is likely to obtain five falsely significant results (Type I errors) in every hundred of such tests: That is the meaning of "$p < .05$." Unfortunately, one never knows when such a result has been obtained. Second, it is highly unlikely that the variables used in a retention study are independent of one another (that is, uncorrelated). Aptitude scores are related to percentile rank in class and to cumulative GPA in college, and these things are associated with race/ethnicity, which, in turn, is related to socioeconomic status of parents, and so on. With repeated bivariate tests of significance on correlated variables, the overlap quickly makes interpretation of the results extremely difficult and uncertain. All we know is that each of two or more variables, taken alone, predicts attrition; no light is shed on whether each variable is needed or, if only one is necessary, which is the best. Such analyses are not only unparsimonious but also virtually uninterpretable with any degree of clarity. As Spady (1970, p. 77) has written, "further. . . bivariate research on the 'correlates' of dropping out should be abandoned. Now!"

The remainder of this section summarizes the advantages and limits of multivariate statistical procedures for analyzing data on problems we know intuitively to be multivariate.

Table 1. Summary Evaluation of Three Designs
for Studying Attrition

Consideration	Autopsy Studies	Cross-Sectional Studies	Longitudinal Studies
Research Considerations			
Instrument reliability[a]	Probably limited	Possible	Possible
Instrument validity[a]	Probably limited	Possible	Possible
Likely response rates	15–40%	55–80%	40–60%[b]
Sample representativeness	Unlikely	More likely	More likely
Internal validity			
Comparisons with non-dropouts	No	Yes	Yes
Controls for initial group differences	No	Limited[c]	Yes
Analytical procedures	Usually descriptive or bivariate	Bivariate or multivariate	Multivariate
Applicability of data to other purposes	None–Limited	Moderate–High	Moderate–High
Planning considerations			
Needed training/experience of project staff	Minimal	Moderate to advanced	Advanced
Time to complete study	3–5 months	6–9 months	15 months
Direct costs (relatively)	Low	Low–Moderate	High
Planning needed	Limited	Limited–Moderate	Considerable
Data-management problems and requirements	Few	Few–Moderate	Many

[a]Depends more on the training and skill of the person(s) designing the study than on the design adopted.
[b]Response rates, expressed as proportions of an initial sample, decline with each subsequent data collection.
[c]Assumes that the only precollege information available for study respondents is typically collected at time of application for admission.

Source: Terenzini, 1980.

Multiple-Regression Approaches. Multiple regression is a statistical procedure by means of which the contributions of multiple independent variables to the prediction of a dependent variable can be estimated both individually (the unique importance of each variable) and in the aggregage (the combined effect, or predictive power, of all independent variables taken together). Kim and Kohout (1975) offer a relatively nontechnical introduction to the topic, and Kerlinger and Pedhazur (1973) present an extended and somewhat more mathematical discussion that is still readable, even for those who have a limited knowledge of statistics.

Virtually all standard statisical computer packages have routines to perform multiple regressions. For example, we might test the following simple model: Attrition/Retention = Gender + Race + Socioeconomic status + SAT scores + High school percentile rank + Faculty contact + College cumulative GPA + Intellectual growth. In this illustration, we are testing the hypothesis that a student's decision to remain in school or to drop out is a function of eight

variables. The task is to identify the best predictors of attendance and to estimate how strongly they are related to decisions to stay or to drop out. Results
of the analysis will include the value of R^2, which will answer the question of
the strength of the relation by giving the proportion of the variance in attendance behavior predictable from the variables included in the model. A significance test of the magnitude of R^2 is part of the standard results in most computer packages.

The question of which variables are the best predictors is illuminated
by examination of the beta weights (standardized regression coefficients). The
relative magnitude of each variable's weight reflects its comparative importance. Therefore, if the weight for gender is twice the magnitude of that for socioeconomic status (SES), then it can be said that gender contributes twice as
much as SES to the explanation of variations in attrition behavior. The signs
of the weights (plus or minus) indicate whether the relation is direct (positive)
or inverse (negative). Formulas for testing the significance of the unique contribution of each variable (while controlling for all other variables in the
model) are given in Kim and Kohout (1975, p. 339) and in Kerlinger and
Pedhazur (1973, p. 70).

Hierarchical-Regression Models. Institutional researchers are familiar
with the "Input-Process-Output" model for conceptualizing and studying programmatic and individual student educational outcomes. Less well known is
the fact that hierarchical regression is ideal for estimating the importance of
individual student and institutional experience variables that might constitute
each of the attrition-related input and process components of this model.

In hierarchical regression, individual variables or sets of variables are
entered into the analysis in a specified, controlled order. For example, let us
assume that we are interested in sources of attrition that are within the institution's sphere of influence — the institutional contribution to attrition. We recognize that the characteristics students bring with them to college can have an
influence on their attendance patterns and that some entering students are
more attrition-prone than others. To address our questions, the model given
earlier can be structured hierarchically by considering gender, race, SES,
SAT scores, and high school percentile rank as the precollege set, and treating
the remaining variables as the college-experience set. The regression analysis
is then conducted in two stages: The precollege-variable set is entered first,
followed by the college-experience variable set. This ordering procedure is
similar to stepwise (as opposed to setwise) regression, in which variables enter
the analysis one at a time, according to some criterion or as specified by the researcher. In the present instance, however, sets of variables are entered in a
specified order, each variable within a set entering at the same time as the others in the set.

Following the entry of all sets (in our example, there were only two),
we can determine the aggregate importance of the college-experience set by
testing the significance of the increase in the value of R^2 from Step 1 to Step 2,
using the formulas given in Kim and Kohout (1975) and in Kerlinger and

Pedhazur (1973). The importance of individual variables can be assessed by examining the beta weights, as in the sample regression model discussed above.

Two of the most prominent theoretical models of student attrition (Spady, 1970; Tinto, 1975) suggest that the same college experiences may affect different students differently, so far as the decision to continue or terminate enrollment is concerned. Such differential patterns of influence for different kinds of students are referred to as "interaction effects." It is quite possible, for example, that male students with low academic aptitudes may respond differently to their college experiences from the way women students with similarly low academic abilities respond. To test whether such differences in reaction might be related to attrition or retention, we can create a new variable within our data if we multiply the sex variable by the value of the academic aptitude variable and then enter the product in the regression analysis, just as we would enter any other variable, but after the original variables have entered the model—the so-called "main effects" variables (see Kerlinger and Pedhazur, 1973, pp. 249–258). Pascarella and Terenzini (1979) and Bean (1980) both offer examples of testing interaction effects in the effort to explain students' attendance decisions. Interactions have proved extremely difficult to replicate, however, and they need to be interpreted carefully.

Regression analysis also has its limitations, however. Throughout this discussion, we have assumed that retention/attrition behavior is a dichotomous variable: All students in the study are presumed to be either persisters or dropouts, with this criterion variable dummy-coded (for example, persisters = 1 and dropouts = 0). If we wish to assess differences among three or more categories of retention/attrition behaviors, then other analytical procedures must be adopted. Moreover, multivariate statistical procedures should not be applied in ignorance of the assumptions underlying them. A discusion of those assumptions is beyond the scope of this chapter, but institutional researchers who are not familiar with multivariate statistics should involve someone with statistical skills in the study. This solution is infinitely preferable to ignoring multivariate techniques in favor of the bivariate techniques with which the researcher may feel more comfortable.

Multivariate Analysis of Variance and Discriminant-Function Analysis. Multivariate analysis of variance (MANOVA) is the multivariate extension of the analysis-of-variance procedure (ANOVA) that we could use to determine whether two or more groups are significantly different from one another on a single, interval- or ratio-scaled, independent variable. With multivariate analysis of variance, however, one tests for reliable differences between or among group means on the basis of multiple independent variables. Like ANOVA solutions, however, MANOVA results tell us only whether two or more groups differ significantly on the basis of multiple variables. No information is provided concerning the magnitude of the difference, whether each group is differentiable from the others, and which of the several independent variables is the most powerful.

Discriminant-function analysis provides much of the information that a MANOVA does not. Although the two procedures are conceptually and mathematically different and are commonly treated as distinct from one another (see Cooley and Lohnes, 1971; Tatsuoka, 1971), statistical computer packages (for example, SPSS and BMD-P) generally have subroutines that perform both analyses in the same run. Huberty (1975, p. 545), however, notes that discriminant-function analysis "is now beginning to be interpreted as a unified approach in the solution of a research problem involving a comparison of two or more populations characterized by multiresponse data." He goes on to summarize four aspects of discriminant-function analysis:

1. *Separation* — determining intergroup significant differences of group centroids (that is, group means in multidimensional space).
2. *Discrimination* — studying group separation with respect to dimensions and to (discriminator) variable contribution to separation.
3. *Estimation* — obtaining estimates of interpopulation distances (between centroids) and of degree or relationship between the response variables and group membership.
4. *Classification* — setting up rules of assigning an individual to one of the predetermined exhaustive populations.

First, the combined MANOVA–discriminant-function analysis results produced by the SPSS or BMD-P packages will indicate whether groups formed, say, according to attendance patterns differ significantly on the basis of a set of variables (this is the "separation" feature of Huberty's taxonomy). The key test statistic is a multivariate F-ratio. Second, the results provide information for judging which dimensions are the strongest contributors to the separation (Huberty's "discrimination") between or among groups. Here, discriminant analysis is analogous to factor analysis, in that one or more uncorrelated dimensions will be identified (not all may be statistically significant). The procedure produces functions (like regression equations) numbering one less than the number of groups or one less than the number of variables, whichever is smaller. Each of these functions is characterized by a set of discriminant weights, or coefficients, which are interpreted like beta weights: The larger the discriminant weight, the more important the variable in differentiating among groups (predicting group membership) along that particular dimension. As in factor analysis, we may label each function, giving it a name to reflect the nature of the large contributors, but recognizing that when we name a discriminant function or a factor, we leave the realm of science and enter the world of art.

Before proceeding, we should note the special case of a discriminant analysis performed with only two groups (say, persisters and dropouts). In this instance, the discriminant weights are proportional to the regression coefficients yielded by a multiple-regression approach in which the dependent variable is dichotomous and dummy-coded (Michael and Perry, 1956); I believe that the regression solution offers more useful results.

Huberty's (1975) third element ("estimation") refers to the fact that the results of a discriminant analysis also permit us to examine the relative locations of each group in the multidimensional space. When two or more statistically significant discriminant functions are produced, it is useful to plot the group centroids (or means), using axes to represent the functions, with each axis at a ninety-degree angle to the others. Knowing the variables that characterize each of the functions, we can then describe how the groups differ from one another and estimate the differences among the groups (see Tatsuoka, 1971, pp. 166–170).

Finally, most computer packages for the social sciences also provide a classification analysis as part of the standard output for their discriminant-function routines. Recall that a multiple-regression equation is a linear combination of independent variables (plus a constant), each weighted according to its importance in predicting some criterion measure. Similarly, each discriminant function is a weighted linear combination of variables, by means of which group membership is predicted. In principle, we might devise one or more discriminant functions capable of differentiating reliably between or among students grouped according to their attendance behaviors, and then we could apply those functions' weights to a single individual's scores on each of the variables to "predict" which attrition/retention group that individual most resembles (see Astin, 1975, pp. 186–194, for an example of a prediction equation derived using multiple regression).

Discriminant-function and classification analysis are more commonly used to "predict" a student's membership in a group to which the student is already known to belong, as a test of the discriminating power of the function produced. Typically, the same students used to derive the function(s) are also used in the classification analysis, producing spuriously high percentages of "correct" classifications.

If at all possible, it is preferable to run the classification analysis on a group of known persisters and dropouts whose scores were not used to derive the discriminant functions. This procedure, called "cross-validation," can be accomplished by randomly dividing each of our attrition groups into, say, halves. For illustrative purposes, assume we have only two groups: leavers and persisters. One might designate a random half of the persisters as "Group 1" and a random half of the leavers as "Group 2." The remaining halves could be designated "Group 3" and "Group 4" (persisters and leavers, respectively). Groups 1 and 2 could then be used as the calibration samples to generate the discriminant function(s), Groups 3 and 4 being withheld from the analysis. When the SPSS DISCRIMINANT routine performs the classification analysis, prediction of group membership will be based on the function(s) produced using Groups 1 and 2, but Groups 3 and 4 will also be classified. The percentage of members of Groups 3 and 4 classified appropriately into Groups 1 or 2 will be the percentage of "correct" cross-validated classifications. As the percentages of these cross-validated classifications depart from chance expectations (50 percent in the two-group case), confidence in the stability and utility of the function(s) will increase. The procedure may also be reversed, using Groups 3 and 4 as the calibration samples and cross-validating with Groups 1 and 2. Referred to as "double cross-validation," this is a decidedly powerful assessment of the stability and discriminating power of the function(s).

Most packaged classification programs allow the user to specify the "prior probabilities" of group membership. Using prior probabilities equal to the relative sizes of the various groups amounts to stacking the deck. The classification analysis will be far more informative if we set the prior probabilities of group membership equal for all groups. Such a procedure has the effect of forcing the classification routine to predict group membership using only the independent variables.

Most statistical computer packages offer the capability of ordering the entry of individual (or sets of) variables in the discriminant analysis. These routines calculate a canonical $R(R_c)$ for each function (the correlation of a function and the grouping variable). R_c can be squared to estimate the variance in attendance behavior explained by each function. Increases in R_c^2 attributable to the entry of another set of variables (say, a set characterizing students' college experiences) can be tested for significance using the same procedure as the increase in R^2 in multiple regression. (In testing the increase in R_c^2, however, the degrees of freedom must take into account not only the number of subjects and variables, but also the number of groups.)

Path Analysis. In a footnote concerning the schematic drawing of his theoretical model of college student dropout, Tinto (1975, p. 94) states that "the lines joining the various elements of the model are not to be taken to represent paths of a path model, [although] it is suggested that path analysis utilizing longitudinal data would indeed be an appropriate technique to study dropout behavior." The method alluded to is described by Kerlinger and Pedhazur (1973, p. 305) as "a method for studying the direct and indirect effects of variables taken as causes [on] variables taken as effects. It is important to note that path analysis is not a method for discovering causes, but a method applied to a causal model formulated by the researcher on the basis of knowledge and theoretical considerations." With path analysis, the direct and indirect effects of each variable on retention/attrition can be assessed using multiple regression and can then be expressed in the form of path coefficients, the magnitudes of which reflect the direct and indirect importance of the variables in the model.

Bean's chapter in this volume has discussed the role of theory in the study of attrition/retention, and the importance of having a theory is never clearer than in the application of path-analytic techniques. The use of a path model requires a priori identification of relevant variables and the specification of the relations among them as causal links leading in unidirectional fashion toward a specified outcome — for present purposes, the student's decision to continue or terminate enrollment.

Even if one never applies path-analytic statistical procedures, however, the application of path-analytic thinking to the design of a study of attrition can be a powerful heuristic device for forcing one to specify (in advance of data collection and analysis) the variables to be measured and the relations presumed to exist among them. Path models require an intellectual clarity and rigor often painfully absent in much attrition research, but such models can only improve attrition studies. Space limitations preclude discussion of the statistical procedures of path analysis (see Duncan, 1966; Kerlinger and Pedhazur, 1973; Land, 1969). Bean (1979, 1980) offers examples of the application of path analysis to the study of attrition.

Conclusions

Before and after the selection of a design and analytical procedures, it is important for researchers and administrators to keep in mind that attrition studies, without exception, are correlational; no causal links can be established, even with path analysis, which merely tests causal relations assumed to exist. The finding that one or more variables are statistically related to attrition or retention is, at best, a statement that the relation is probably not due to chance, as well as a statement about how strong the relation may be; it is not a statement of cause and effect. For the present, at least, the establishment of causal links in the attrition/retention process is beyond our research capabilities.

While no retention study design or set of analytical procedures is without its drawbacks, it seems reasonably clear that certain approaches or methods have more to offer than others. The autopsy design, for example, appears to have little to recommend it other than its simplicity and comparatively low price. By contrast, the longitudinal or panel study plan carries with it considerable promise for sufficient data (collected at important times) leading to potentially important useful knowledge about what we may sense intuitively to be a complex problem, both conceptually and methodologically. Such information comes at a comparatively high price, however.

Similar sorts of tradeoffs are required in the selection of data-collection and data-analysis procedures. If it is clear that the autopsy design by itself has little to recommend it, then it is also clear that repeated bivariate statistical procedures are equally bankrupt. They may be widely familiar, but the information they yield is likely to be confounded and will possibly do more harm than good, depending on administrative actions that may be based on it.

The selection of data-collection and data-analysis designs and procedures must also be considered in light of human and financial costs likely to be incurred. The matter is not simply one of adding up the costs associated with the study itself. Assuming that the study attracts some administrative attention and action (see the chapter by Beal and Pascarella in this volume), we must also take into account the possible costs of administrative actions and program development that may follow on the results of an attrition study. It is, finally, institutional researchers and administrators who must strike and then live with the balance between desirable design and analytical approaches, on the one hand, and available resources, on the other.

References

Astin, A. W. *Preventing Students from Dropping Out.* San Francisco: Jossey-Bass, 1975.

Bean, J. P. "Path Analysis: The Development of a Suitable Methodology for the Study of Student Attrition." Paper presented to the annual conference of the American Educational Research Association, San Francisco, April 1979.

Bean, J. P. "Dropouts and Turnover: The Synthesis and Test of a Causal Model of Student Attrition." *Research in Higher Education,* 1980, *12,* 155–187.

Bower, C., and Meyers, E. A. *A Manual for Conducting Student Attrition Studies in Institutions of Postsecondary Education.* Technical Report No. 74. Boulder, Colo.: National Center for Higher Education Management Systems, 1976.

Campbell, D. T., and Stanley, J. C. *Experimental and Quasi-Experimental Designs for Research.* Chicago: Rand McNally, 1963.

Cooley, W. W., and Lohnes, P. R. *Multivariate Data Analysis.* New York: Wiley, 1971.

Cope, R., and Hannah, W. *Revolving College Doors: The Causes and Consequences of Dropping Out, Stopping Out, and Transferring.* New York: Wiley–Interscience, 1975.

Duncan, O. D. "Path Analysis: Sociological Examples." *The American Journal of Sociology,* 1966, *72,* 1–16.

Fenstemacher, W. P. *College Dropouts: Theories and Research Findings.* St. Paul: Minnesota State College System, 1973.

Huberty, C. J. "Discriminant Analysis." *Review of Educational Research,* 1975, *45,* 543–598.

Kerlinger, F. N. *Foundations of Behavioral Research.* (2nd ed.) New York: Holt, Rinehart and Winston, 1973.

Kerlinger, F. N., and Pedhazur, E. J. *Multiple Regression in Behavioral Research.* New York: Holt, Rinehart and Winston, 1973.

Kim, J., and Kohout, F. J. "Multiple Regression Analysis: Subprogram Regression." In N. H. Nie and others (Eds.), *SPSS: Statistical Package for the Social Sciences.* (2nd ed.) New York: McGraw-Hill, 1975.

Land, K. C. "Principles of Path Analysis." In E. F. Borgatta (Ed.), *Sociological Methodology.* San Francisco: Jossey-Bass, 1969.

Michael, W. B., and Perry, N. C. "The Comparability of the Simple Discriminant Function and Multiple Regression Techniques." *Journal of Experimental Education,* 1956, *24,* 297–301.

Pantages, T. J., and Creedon, C. F. "Studies of College Attrition: 1950–1975." *Review of Educational Research,* 1978, *48,* 49–101.

Pascarella, E. T., and Terenzini, P. T. "Interaction Effects in Spady's and Tinto's Conceptual Models of College Dropout." *Sociology of Education,* 1979, *52,* 197–210.

Spady, W. "Dropouts from Higher Education: An Interdisciplinary Review and Synthesis." *Interchange,* 1970, *1,* 109–121.

Tatsuoka, M. M. *Multivariate Analysis: Techniques for Educational and Psychological Research.* New York: Wiley, 1971.

Terenzini, P. T. "An Evaluation of Three Basic Designs for Studying Attrition." *Journal of College Student Personnel,* 1980, *21,* p. 259.

Tinto, V. "Dropout from Higher Education: A Theoretical Synthesis of Recent Research." *Review of Educational Research,* 1975, *45,* 89–125.

Patrick T. Terenzini is director of institutional research and associate professor of education at the State University of New York at Albany. His research interests include the study of attrition and the impacts of college on students.

Existing programs designed to influence student retention are
discussed, and a procedure for verifying their effects is presented.

Designing Retention Interventions and Verifying Their Effectiveness

Philip Beal
Ernest T. Pascarella

The immediate and long-term costs of student attrition, particularly when viewed against current economic and demographic trends, have led to increased interest in programs that positively influence student retention. A surprising number of these programs have been implemented in postsecondary institutions, with varying levels of success. The purpose of this chapter is twofold. First, we shall provide a description of existing programs designed to improve student retention. This description will focus on perceived impact, reasons for success or failure, and impediments to progress in carrying out retention programs. While there are a number of significant impediments to progress in carrying out programs designed to improve student retention, one that falls most directly within the activities of institutional researchers is the lack of thorough evaluation. The second purpose of this chapter, therefore, will be to present an analytical model for verifying the effectiveness of retention-improvement programs that institutional researchers may wish to consider.

Programs Designed to Improve Student Rentention

At least one institutional rationale for retention programs is self-evident: Bibliographies attached to recent publications cite studies and articles

E. Pascarella (Ed.). *New Directions for Institutional Research: Studying Student Attrition*, no. 35.
San Francisco: Jossey-Bass, December 1982.

in the hundreds scrutinizing the comings, goings, and stayings of college students; the most crucial factor appears to be enrollment and what it makes possible by way of budgets, staffing, credit hours, course sections, and support of services.

Oddly enough, 1981 fall enrollment set a record, according to a recent article (Magarrell, 1981). According to the article, however, the increases were due almost entirely to enrollment gains in two-year colleges. Gains occurring in universities and other four-year institutions were mainly in full-time women students with a dropoff in part-time men and women students, except at private four-year colleges. Thus, while increases in enrollment are taking place, they are not occurring at those institutions that have seemed to show the greatest interest or need for student retention. If enrollment is a major driving force behind student retention, it would seem that most institutions would (or should) be heavily engaged in renewed efforts and strategies designed to keep students enrolled.

The problem with such an assumption is that the educational function of institutions and the role of educators may be lost in the numbers game — lost, that is, unless student retention itself is guided by a consciousness of quality regarding both academic programs and the delivery of services. This consciousness should start with student-institutional fit and how the school reinforces the appropriateness of that fit for students. It extends through classroom experiences, including students' perceptions that faculty members are interested in individual learning. It also involves an institution-wide commitment to high-quality services that assist and challenge the educational awareness of the student.

Our role as educators is to develop in students a self-conscious awareness of quality received that firms their commitment to higher education — ideally, at the institution of choice. If students know that what they are getting is valuable and of high quality, an institution will more closely approximate its own desirable level of retention, whatever that level may be.

The ultimate purpose of retention studies and programs is to implement intervention strategies that can or will make a positive difference in retention rates. Regrettably, much of the existing research has stopped short of action recommendations, emphasizing instead the characteristics of persisters versus dropouts or the difference in retention rates among students compared on any number of variables. By the late 1970s, as reported in Beal and Noel (1980), only a handful of publications had reported on the results of specific intervention strategies. Many colleges, of course, have engaged in retention programs, but the results have never been published or shared with others. Beal and Noel attempted to catalog the nature of retention programs that were under way and to assess their effectiveness in improving retention. Over 900 institutions participated in the study, and 300 of them submitted a total of more than 1,000 written reports describing their retention programs. This chapter will include the results of a follow-up survey of those retention programs noted in Beal and Noel as being the most effective in improving student retention or in having the greatest general impact on the campus. Also included will be a discussion of problems related to conducting effective retention programs. Finally, we shall offer a statement on the need for verifying the results of experimental interventions that are intended to improve student retention, and we shall provide a straightforward analytic method for doing so.

What Is Being Done in the Literature

Several recent publications have offered suggestions about areas of intervention for improved retention. Henderson (1980) reported on selected case studies of specific action programs, including a counseling program at Drake University, expanded work-study and advising at the University of Massachusetts at Boston, follow-up contacts at Fort Hayes State University, and personal and career counseling for freshment dropout risks at Delaware State University. Lenning, Sauer, and Beal (1980) reviewed Beal and Noel (1980), as well as many additional references and recommended student service and academic programs by which retention could be enhanced. In a College Board report, Ramist (1981) encouraged increased retention by enhancing preenrollment, admissions, and orientation programs; providing financial aid and academic counseling, advising, and career-development services; encouraging dormitory residence and student-faculty interaction; fostering participation in campus activities; and requiring exit interviews Another recent publication reviewed studies conducted in order to validate Tinto's (1975) model of college student attrition (Terenzini and Pascarella, 1980). According to Tinto's model, the greater the degree of integration into the college, the greater will be the student's commitment to the specific institution and to the goal of completing higher education. The report reviewed six studies that verified the usefulness of Tinto's model in understanding the dynamics of attrition. The studies supported the role of social and academic integration as being significantly related to leaving and staying. Similar findings were made by Bean (1980), who learned that institutional commitment was a primary variable significantly related to retention. Bean found that the two most important variables influencing institutional commitment were institutional quality and transfer opportunity. Bean also noted that the perceived quality of education is one of the most important variables in influencing institutional commitment, and he offered several suggestions for enhancing institutional commitment. Finally, the impact of learning-assistance programs on student retention was discussed by Beal (1980). Nineteen specific examples are cited of learning centers and learning-assistance programs that have made a positive difference in student retention.

What Works in Student Retention Follow-Up

Beal and Noel (1980) emphasized the action programs that were rated as being most successful in improving student retention and in having a general impact on the campus (see Table 1). After eliminating the duplication of programs that were highly rated both in retention and in general impact, 187 programs were sent a follow-up survey in the fall of 1981 to ascertain their current status and continuing effectiveness. Fifty-nine surveys were returned, for a return rate of 32 percent. Of the programs returned, 32 (54 percent) had been rated as improving retention by four or more percentage points (an index of 4 or 5) and 48 (81 percent) had been rated as having a significant impact (an index of 5) on the campus. Table 1 shows the original action programs of Beal and Noel (1980) and the breakdown of programs included in the follow-up returns. Some of the program categories were not represented by the returns, but in most other cases the programs returned approximated the percentages reported in Beal and Noel. Peer programs were represented in the follow-up sample to a greater extent than in the original study.

Current Status. Most of the programs that responded still existed two years later, with 58 percent continuing in the same form, 34 percent continuing in a modified form, and 8 percent cancelled. Reasons cited for cancellation included faculty boredom, attained goals, lack of funding, and changes in staff assignments. Modifications to programs generally involved expansion to a wider target group. These changes included requiring advising for all freshmen, instead of for just those students who had been in academic difficulty; providing for individual contact with students; expanding the number of sections of special courses; using more students as paraprofessionals; developing

Table 1. Action Programs of Retention Leaders and Follow-up
(Reported in Percentages)

	Original Study		Follow-Up	
	Retention	*General*	*Retention*	*General*
1. Advising	14	17	16	15
2. Learning/Academic support	31	24	38	25
3. Orientation	20	15	16	15
4. Career assistance	6	8	0	4
5. Counseling	4	2	0	2
6. Exit interviews	0	0	0	0
7. Peer programs	1	8	3	17
8. Early-warning systems	13	6	16	4
9. New policies and structures	4	4	3	2
10. Dropout studies	3	1	3	2
11. Faculty–staff development	1	5	3	6
12. Cocurricular activities	1	1	0	0
13. Curricular developments	1	2	0	0
14. Multiple-action programs	3	6	3	4
15. Other	1	3	0	4
N	110	149	32	38
N less duplications	187		59	

Source: Beal & Noel (1980).

better data systems; reducing staff due to funding difficulties, and introducing greater emphasis on career counseling.

Impact on Retention. Most of the respondents (90 percent) indicated that their programs still had a positive impact on retention and/or a positive general impact on the campus, but very few of the schools engaged in evaluations sufficient to determine the effectiveness of their programs with scientific certainty. A percentage analysis of students retained over previous years, or of performance versus previous performance, was used by 22 percent of the schools. Only four of the schools (7 percent) conducted studies using control groups along with experimental groups. A number of respondents suggested that they perceived a positive impact on the campus although they could not document the results (12 percent). In 6 percent of the cases, respondents used subjective evaluations (surveys of students and ratings by faculty) to evaluate program effectiveness. One respondent reported constantly evaluating the retention effort, and another reported tracking each student.

A review of the written responses leaves little doubt that the respondents were well satisfied with their efforts and felt that retention improvement had taken place. In some cases the percentage of improvement was dramatic. The value of applying sophisticated assessment techniques to retention programs will be discussed later in this chapter; suffice it to say now that most institutions could probably be more deliberate and thorough in their program evaluations. In the meantime, however, the follow-up survey supports the Beal and Noel findings: Intervention strategies are associated with improved student retention, and such improvements seem to persist over a period of time.

Reasons for Success or Failure. The top five reasons respondents gave for the success of their programs were staff quality, administrative leadership, faculty involvement, use of students as peer participants, and inservice training. While not to be discounted as an important ingredient in successful programs, funding was mentioned considerably less often. Funding was mentioned as critical, however, in the cancellation of several programs. Thus, while funding may not be necessary for a particular program on a given campus, many successful programs either had adequate funding or did not need much funding to be effective.

Written comments by the respondents amplified the reasons for success. Most striking, perhaps, by the number of comments made was the value of peer participants in a variety of programs, including advising, learning assistance, orientation, and peer programs for early warning. Also of striking importance was faculty involvement, along with inservice training for faculty members to help make them effective. Involvement and cooperation with various departments across campus were mentioned as important; one program emphasized the value of an advisory committee from across campus, which assisted with a learning-assistance program. Another respondent stressed that the staff must be competent, sensitive, patient, and personable, with a genuine interest in students' welfare. While that comment was made in reference to a learning-assistance program, it may well identify the most important ingredients for success in any program.

Difficulties. The single most common difficulty mentioned in the open-ended question on the survey was funding, although not many respondents elaborated on their specific problems. One respondent said the school offered no incentives for advisors to increase their efforts. The next most common difficulty experienced in the programs was lack of time for both staff implementation and administrative leadership. A number of comments were made about the difficulty of maintaining consistent faculty effort, often because of inadequate time and inservice training or lack of motivation. Some respondents mentioned resistance to learning-assistance programs from faculty who did not accept the legitimacy of underprepared students within the college, or from students who resented being designated as special risks. One respondent reported that the faculty was unenthusiastic about special-risk groups and that some instructors preferred to believe there were no such students, or that they should not have been admitted. Another respondent mentioned that such resistance existed only until the value of the program became evident. Finally, several comments were made to the effect that students did not seem to accept responsibility for their own behavior or performance and therefore did not respond well to the efforts to assist them.

New Programs. Quite a number of respondents have provided information about new programs that have been generated since the original questionnaire. Virtually all the new programs under way have similarities to the programs already referenced in Beal and Noel (1980) and in many other publications. No college, of course, should be encouraged simply to adopt a program that seems to be effective elsewhere. Nevertheless, a college could select one, two, or three that seem appropriate and implement a version addressing particular needs. Regrettably, some institutions do not benefit from programs under way elsewhere. Even though unique institutional characteristics do exist, potential areas for intervention seem to follow similar patterns, which should be adaptable to almost all institutions with similar needs.

General Comments on the Need for Student Retention. One of the open-ended questions on the survey asked for general comments on the feasibility and legitimacy of student retention efforts on campuses today. Many respondents supplied answers to this question; all endorsed the desirability of retention efforts, and many did so with most vigorous language. Probably the most common concern mentioned by the respondents (besides the importance of engaging in student retention efforts) was the need to maintain academic standards and instructional quality. Concern for appropriate college–student fit was frequently mentioned; as one respondent said, "There can be no more legitimate pursuit than student retention — so long as college is the right place for the student — and retention efforts should always include honest, forthright appraisal of the student's chance of success and happiness at an institution. Retention efforts are the duty of an institution."

Colleges are concerned about the increasing number of students who are underprepared for college work, either because of inadequate basic skills or inadequate motivation. As one respondent put it, "We need to do a better job of bringing these students up to our standards, or else we will be guilty of a 'ripoff,' by misrepresenting their chances just to get them admitted." Other concerns involved the need for administrative and faculty support of the retention concept, with collegewide participation. To show evidence of that support, there should be specific assignment of responsibility to an individual with sufficient influence to make changes.

An underlying theme of many of the comments was the critical problem of maintaining enrollment. Several respondents referred to the importance of retention for sustaining enrollment, as opposed to the unrealistic approach of continually recruiting more students. Other respondents indicated that retention could not be a goal in and of itself; rather, retention should be the result of improvement in services and the overall quality of the institution. Finally, it should always be recognized that some attrition is both necessary and desirable. Part of the the goal of a retention program should be to help students identify what is best for them, including another institution, other endeavors, or employment.

Impediments to Progress

When this outline developed, it was anticipated that very specific difficulties or impediments to progress could be identified that, if addressed, would help institutions achieve success. Instead, the primary difficulties faced by institutions implementing retention efforts seem to be reducible to only three major factors—commitment, organization, and documentation.

Commitment. The importance of commitment to any endeavor is readily understood, but as related to student retention, commitment may show some unique variations. The following statements may summarize why commitment may be difficult to attain on any particular campus:

1. As long as admissions are strong, we don't have to worry.
2. The sanctity of empires needs to be protected—we're doing great anyway.
3. Students who can't cut it, or who otherwise should not be here, should leave.
4. Retention efforts will not receive recognition or reward, and so we cannot commit the time and effort to do it.
5. Our job is to teach, or to administer, or to serve a specific function; retention belongs somewhere else.
6. It costs too much.
7. Time commitments and priorities of presidents lie in other areas.
8. After all, we do not want to lower our standards.

Each of the above statements includes an element of valid concern, which needs to be addressed. For programs to be successful, the prospect of resistance must be accepted as normal—necessary, in fact—to an effective program that will eventually receive support from the whole campus. Addressing the problem of resistance, however, demands commitment.

Organization. Only brief comments will be suggested regarding organization. For retention efforts to be successful, particularly if change is involved, several basic organizational principles need to be followed, starting with specific assignment of responsibilities and performance expectations. Participation of all potential implementers must be included, as well as that of intended program recipients. High-risk students, minority students, handicapped students, and freshmen can all make suggestions for program design.

While slavish adherence to a management-by-objectives approach is not necessary, any program still needs to have fairly clear goals and a fairly clear system for determining whether goals are met. A reward system is highly desirable; even in days of tight funding and inadequate resources, creative means can be devised for recognizing a job well done.

Documentation and Evaluation. The final impediment to progress we shall discuss in this context is lack of both documentation and evaluation. Suffice it to say here that an institution must know what it is doing and have the means to evaluate the retention process, as well as the results. Without minimizing the many good efforts reported in the recent survey as well as in Beal and Noel (1980), we ask: How much more impact would many of the programs have if efforts were documented and evaluated, if for no other reason than to support renewed funding in the future? Priorities for the educational dollar are constantly being shifted. What better way could money be spent than to enhance the educational health and vitality of an institution, as measured through student retention?

Going in New Directions

One of the strong impressions to be gained from looking at so many examples of retention efforts is how often colleges are bent on reinventing the wheel. Many campus studies are started from scratch, and many others are duplicated, but all could benefit from efforts between or among campuses. If, as so many believe, retention is only the byproduct of improved services and instruction, might there not be ways in which cooperative efforts could accomplish the same ends?

Once students are enrolled, the object is to offer a quality education. Program improvements at one college need not compete with those at other colleges, particularly in areas of student service. Cooperative efforts could be made among several colleges to offer inservice training on improved advising for faculty. Teams of representatives from several colleges might assist each other with faculty development and instructional innovation. Colleges might share data to devise programs for tracking students and use computer services that can serve more than one institution.

Since staff quality is so important to the success of programs, training and development of staff could be handled cooperatively in a number of areas, including orientation, learning assistance, counseling, and employing of students as paraprofessionals. Funding sources could be even more amenable to program suggestions that can benefit several colleges at once, either in a given region or across a broader geographic area. Perhaps the new direction for student retention is to increase awareness of the possibilities for interinstitutional cooperation.

Student retention is not a panacea for enrollment problems. Even if effective programs are in place, students will still withdraw from institutions. Nevertheless, concerted efforts toward student retention can involve institutions in a disciplined investigation of their own educational practices, and such efforts are important enough to warrent rigorous evaluation.

Verifying the Effectiveness of Retention Improvement Programs

Spady (1970), Tinto (1975), and others seem generally to agree that a primary weakness of most attrition research is the lack of a theoretical rationale to guide the selection of the student and college-experience variables employed to predict persistence/withdrawal decisions. Similarly, it is likely that a major weakness in many interventions designed to reduce attrition is the failure to be guided by the consistently significant correlates of student persistence/withdrawal.

Clearly, the underlying rationale for any experimental intervention is that the particular treatment received will have a direct or indirect effect on persistence. While a statistically reliable correlation between two variables does not necessarily indicate a causal relationship, whenever two variables are causally related there will always be an accompanying nonzero correlation between them. (Conversely, the lack of a nonzero correlation between two variables generally rules out the presence of a causal relationship). The large and growing body of correlational studies on attrition can provide valuable guidance in identifying areas of student life (for example, residence arrangements, nonclassroom interaction with the faculty) that may causally influence the persistence/withdrawal process. These areas of the college experience can then be tested for their degree of causal influence on persistence through the more vigorous criterion of the manipulated field experiment.

What we are suggesting here in nothing more than a coordinated, sequential use of both correlational and experimental methods in attrition research at the institutional level. The first step is to identify the areas of student life at an institution that are significantly associated with persistence. The second step is to use the data yielded by correlational studies as a guide in developing specific or programmatic interventions designed to influence persistence positively. The final step is to test the effectivenss of these programmatic interventions experimentally.

Verifying the Experimental Intervention

In their landmark discussion of experimental and quasiexperimental designs, Campbell and Stanley (1963) introduced the concepts of "internal" and "external" validity. Briefly, internal validity is the extent to which we can say that the independent variable (usually our manipulated intervention) is solely responsible for the average differences noted between experimental and control groups on the dependent variable. External validity, in contrast, is the extent to which we can generalize the results of the experiment to other contexts or subject populations.

Clearly, the primary concern of most experimental designs in the social sciences has been internal validity. Indeed, the essential characteristics of a true experiment (a manipulated independent variable with at least one group of subjects receiving the treatment and one group not receiving it, and random assignment of subjects to experimental and control conditions) are designed to eliminate the various threats to internal validity (for example, history, differential mortality, selection bias, and regression artifacts). It is hazardous to judge an intervention's effectiveness in the absence of evaluation designs that have, at a minimum, an experimental group receiving the intervention and a control group of reasonably similar students who are not receiving the intervention.

While internal validity is a necessary condition, it is not likely in and of itself to be a sufficient condition for evaluating the effectiveness of retention programs, even within a single institution, where generalizability (external validity) is less of a concern. The reason for this is that we can have good internal validity in an evaluation design and still know very little about the extent to which the intervention or treatment was implemented as proposed. When this occurs, a number of questions remain unanswered: If the results are statistically significant, what aspects of the treatment accounted for effects observed? (This concern may be particularly important in retention interventions, since such interventions are likely to be multi- rather than unidimensional.) If the results are not statistically significant, is it because the intervention had no effect? Or is it simply because the intervention never really occurred as intended? Cook and Campbell (1979) refer to these issues under the broad heading of "experimental construct validity." We shall refer to them more simply as a problem of verifying interventions.

A Model for Verifying Retention Interventions

We offer the following analytic model as a method for verifying programmatic interventions designed to increase student retention. (It is assumed that the design of the evaluation is either a true experiment or a quasiexperiment.) The model draws heavily on the thinking of Hall and Loucks (1977) and Leinhardt (1980) and has four steps or stages: (1) operationally defining and measuring the intended dimensions or processes of the intervention, (2) determining if the independent variable (typically a dummy-coded variable with 1 representing membership in the experimental group and 0 representing membership in the control group) is significantly associated with the intended dimensions of the intervention, (3) determining if the independent variable (or intervention) is significantly associated with the outcome measure (for example, institutional persistence versus withdrawal), and (4) determining if those intended dimensions of the intervention associated with the independent variable account for the effects of the independent variable on the outcome measure.

An Empirical Example

Perhaps the easiest way of understanding the model is by illustrating its application with an actual data-based example (Pascarella and Terenzini, 1980). A large, private residential university was concerned with improving the intellectual and cultural quality of freshman-year residential life. Based in part on the evidence from existing research on college impacts, it was decided that one way to accomplish this goal was to increase the role and influence of the institution's faculty in student residence facilities. To this end, an experimental living-learning residence (LLR) was developed. In addition to a number of other features, it included seven live-in academic staff members; a faculty lecture series on current topics; an extensive series of credit and noncredit courses taught in the LLR; and a series of regularly scheduled informal discussion sessions with facuty, deans, university administrators, and visiting scholars. It was expected that the LLR structure would foster the growth of a distinctive set of influential interpersonal relationships, primarily between students and faculty members, but also among the students living in the LLR. It was further expected that participation in the LLR would be associated with some desirable educational outcomes, including increased student intellectual and personal development, as well as freshman-to-sophomore–year persistence.

To test this general set of expectations or hypotheses, a quasiexperiment was conducted, which compared a random sample of freshmen living in the experimental LLR with a random sample of freshmen living in conventional (control group) residences. Because freshmen could not be randomly assigned to experimental and control groups (which would have made the design a true experiment), multiple-regression procedures were used to statistically control student differences in a battery of fifteen background/ precollege characteristics (for example, race, academic aptitude, secondary-school achievement, educational aspirations, and college expectations).

Given this background, we come to Step 1 of the model — operationally defining and measuring the intended dimensions or processes of the intervention. Since the LLR was expected to foster a distinctive set of influential student–faculty and student–student relationships, a series of five-response Likert scales ("strongly agree" to "strongly disagree") was developed to assess the quality and impact of these relationships. The scales were termed *peer-group interactions* ('My interpersonal relationships with other students have had a positive influence on my intellectual growth and interest in ideas"); *interactions with faculty* ("My nonclassroom interactions with faculty have had a positive influence on my personal growth, values, and attitudes"); and *faculty concern for teaching and student development* ("Few of the faculty members I have had contact with are willing to spend time outside of class to discuss issues of interest and importance to students" — reverse-coded). If the LLR were implemented as intended, then it would be expected that students in the LLR would have significantly higher scores on all three scales. In this case, the first step of the model would be one whereby the investigator would define operationally those dimensions or processes to be used subsequently as evidence that the intervention (LLR) was implemented as intended.

The second step in the model would be to verify the intervention by determining whether being exposed (versus not being exposed) to the intervention would be associated with measures of its intended dimensions or processes. In our example study, this entailed solving the following regression equation:

$$P_i = \text{Background} + EI,$$

where P_i is any one particular process dimension of the intervention. Background represents the battery of fifteen preenrollment characteristics. EI is the dummy-coded independent variable (1 = LLR students; 0 = control residence students) representing the overall experimental intervention versus exposure to the control condition.

The equation statistically controls the influence of the fifteen student background traits and provides an estimate of the association between the dummy independent variable (that is, the LLR versus control residences) and each of the three scales representing the dimensions of the intervention. (This type of analysis is also known as the analysis of covariance.) With the battery of student background characteristics held constant, the dummy variable representing the experimental intervention (versus control residences) had a statistically significant, positive partial correlation with each of the three scales — peer-group interactions, interactions with faculty, and faculty concern for teaching and student development. The LLR students had significantly higher mean scores on all three variables than did the control students. Such evidence would tend to verify that, in terms of fostering a set of student-faculty and student–peer relationships different in quality and influence from those occurring for students in conventional residences, the LLR was implemented as intended.

The third step in the model would be to determine whether the dummy variable representing the intervention is significantly associated with the intended outcomes. This can be operationally defined by the following regression equation:

$$\text{Outcome} = \text{Background} + EI,$$

where the only new term, *outcome,* is the dependent measure or measures. This is often the only analysis conducted in the vast majority of experimental studies. Unfortunately, such an analysis merely suggests whether or not there is an overall composite effect due to the intervention; it does little to identify which aspects of the intervention may have accounted for the effects observed.

In the example investigation, there were eight outcome measures — freshman year academic achievement, two measures of intellectual and personal development, four measures of campus environmental press, and freshman-to-sophomore–year persistence versus voluntary withdrawal decisions. For purposes of illustration and simplicity, we shall limit our discussion to persistence/withdrawal decisions. With differences in background characteristics held constant statistically, the LLR students as a group were found to have a significantly higher rate of freshman-to-sophomore–year persistence than students in the control residences. While this was welcome news, it indicated only that the overall environment of the LLR (represented by the dummy treatment variable) had a positive influence on persistence. It did not suggest which particular dimensions of the LLR accounted for this influence. To shed light on the latter issue, we must extend the analysis to the final step of the model.

The fourth and final step in the model would be to determine whether the intended dimensions of the intervention account for the effects of the independent variable (LLR versus control residences) on the outcome measure. This is the most complicated part of the analysis and can be illustrated best by the following simplified regression equation:

$$\text{Outcome} = \text{Background} + (P_1 + P_2 \ldots P_n) + EI$$

where $P_1 + P_2 \ldots P_n$ represent the verified process dimensions of the intervention. In the present study, these were the three scales assessing the quality and influence of relationships with faculty and peers.

In the actual regression analysis, the variable sets on the right-hand side of the equation would be entered in the following sequential order: (1) background characteristics; (2) $P_1 P_2 \ldots P_n$; and (3) EI. Thus, with background characteristics held constant, we could first determine whether those process dimensions of the intervention (verified in Step 2 of the model) might be significantly associated with the dependent measure. This is important, in that it suggests which particular processes $(P_1 P_2 \ldots P_n)$ fostered by the experimental intervention might have a significant, positive influence on intended outcomes.

Subsequently, the investigator could determine whether the process dimensions of the experimental intervention might account for the effect of the intervention on the outcome measure by adding the dummy variable (representing exposure to the experimental intervention or control condition) to the third regression equation (above). If the process dimensions $(P_1 P_2 \ldots P_n)$ did in fact account for the composite influence of the intervention, then the significant effect of the dummy variable (representing composite intervention effects) in the equation

$$\text{Outcome} = \text{Background} + EI$$

would become nonsignificant in the equation

$$\text{Outcome} = \text{Background} + (P_1 + P_2 \ldots P_n) + EI$$

In short, since measures of the important process dimensions of the intervention are represented in the equation, they should account for nearly all the composite intervention effect represented by the dummy variable.

In the example study, with background characteristics held constant, the three process dimensions of the LLR (the student–faculty and student–peer relationship scales) each had significant ($p < .01$), positive regression weights with freshman-to-sophomore–year persistence. (The standardized regression [beta] weights for interactions with faculty [.203] and faculty concern for teaching and student development [.211] scales were about twice as large as the weight [.104] for the peer-group interactions scale, indicating about twice the relative unique influence on persistence.) Furthermore, when the dummy variable (representing the overall effects of the LLR) was added to the equation containing both the background variables and the three process dimension, it was no longer statistically significant. (Recall that the dummy variable *was* significantly related to persistence in Step 2 of the model, when background variables alone were held constant.) We concluded that the three measures of student–faculty and student–peer relationships captured all the significant effects of exposure to the LLR on freshman-to-sophomore–year persistence. Had the dummy variable still been significant, it would have suggested that the three process dimensions did not account for the total positive effect of the LLR on persistence.

Caveats and Recommendations

We believe the four-step model introduced and illustrated above has several distinct advantages in studying the effects of any programmatic intervention on student retention. First, by requiring that the underlying process dimensions of the intervention be specified and operationally defined, the model forces the investigator to consider in some detail exactly why the intervention should have the particular influence on student persistence that it does. Second, the model requires the intervention to be empirically verified in terms of the particular processes that it fosters, permitting a determination of the extent to which the intervention was implemented as intended. Finally, the analytical procedures of the model focus not simply on the gross effects of a programmatic intervention but, rather, on the extent to which the specific underlying processes of the program account for its overall influence on retention. Such evidence may be particularly useful in identifying those specific components of a program that have the greatest impact on desired outcomes.

As with any analytical method, the usefulness of the results, in terms of both theoretical and policy implications, depends most heavily on the quality of the data employed and the care with which the evaluation is conducted. Obviously, considerable care and thought must attend the operational definition and measurement of the process dimensions of the programmatic intervention. Before substantial human and fiscal resources are invested in any large intervention designed to improve student retention, however, it would probably be wise to pilot the program on a small scale first. This permits investigators to identify and work out the "bugs" that inevitably occur the first time any complex program is implemented. The first two steps of the model can be quite useful at the pilot stage for determining those components of the intervention that were implemented as intended and those that were not. It may make more sense to worry about the effects of the intervention on student retention only after there is some reasonable assurance that the intervention is being conducted as planned.

In terms of the dependent measure, we have stressed student persistence versus withdrawal. It is important, however, to maintain sensitivity to ancillary or unintended outcomes of programmatic interventions aimed at influencing retention. It may be, for example, that a particular programmatic intervention exhibits no direct effects on student persistence, but influences such ancillary areas as intellectual development, personal development, study skills, or career aspirations; and since any of these factors may positively influence persistence, it would be premature to conclude that the intervention was totally unsuccessful. By directly and positively influencing such intervening or mediating variables, the intervention may have a positive but indirect influence on student persistence. To assess these potential ancillary or indirect effects, it is necessary to consider multiple outcomes, rather than focusing solely on differences in persistence rates.

Finally, a word needs to be added about employing analytical models (such as the one introduced above) in actual research or evaluation projects. The model should be seen as a general guide, rather than as a prescriptive formula. Given the untidy world of program implementation and data collection with human subjects, it is usually much more difficult to apply a model specifically than it is to describe it generally. In addition to the example investigation by Pascarella and Terenzini (180), we would suggest investigations by Lacy (1978) and White, Pascarella and Pflaum (1981) as other examples of how the model has been applied in diverse research contexts.

References

Beal, P. E. "Learning Centers and Retention." In O. Lenning and R. Nayman (Eds.), *New Directions for College Learning Assistance: New Roles for Learning Assistance,* no. 2. San Francisco: Jossey-Bass, 1980.

Beal, P. E., and Noel, L. *What Works in Student Retention.* Iowa City, Iowa, and Boulder, Colo.: American College Testing Program and National Center for Higher Education Management Systems, 1980.

Bean, J. P. "Dropouts and Turnovers: The Synthesis and Test of a Causal Model of Student Attrition." *Research in Higher Education,* 1980, *12* (2), 155–187.

Campbell, D., and Stanley, J. *Experimental and Quasiexperimental Designs for Research.* Chicago: Rand McNally, 1963.

Cook, T., and Campbell, D. *Quasi-Experimentation: Design and Analysis Issues for Field Settings.* Chicago: Rand McNally, 1979.

Hall, G., and Loucks, S. "A Developmental Model for Determining Whether the Treatment Is Actually Implemented." *American Educational Research Journal,* 1977, *14,* 263–276.

Henderson, C. "Retention Improvement: Selected Case Studies." Policy Brief, American Council on Education, December 1980.

Lacy, W. "Interpersonal Relationships as Mediators of Structural Effects: College Student Socialization in a Traditional and an Experimental University Environment." *Sociology of Education,* 1978, *51,* 201–211.

Leinhardt, G. "Modeling and Measuring Educational Treatment in Evaluation." *Review of Education Research,* 1980, *50,* 393–420.

Lenning, O. T., Sauer, K., and Beal, P. E. *Student Retention Strategies.* AAHE/ERIC Higher Education Research Report No. 8, 1980.

Magarrell, J. "Fall Enrollments Set a Record; Large Gains at Two-Year Colleges." *Chronicle of Higher Education,* 1981, *23,* p. 1.

Pascarella, E., and Terenzini, P. "Student–Faculty and Student–Peer Relationships as Mediators of the Structural Effects of Undergraduate Residence Arrangement." *Journal of Educational Research,* 1980, *73,* 344–353.

Ramist, L. *College Student Attrition and Retention.* College Board Report, no. 81-1, College Entrance Examination Board, 1981.

Spady, W. "Dropouts From Higher Education: An Interdisciplinary Review and Synthesis," *Interchange,* 1970, *1,* 109–121.

Terenzini, P. T., and Pascarella, E. T., "Toward the Validation of Tinto's Model of College Student Attrition: A Review of Recent Studies." *Research in Higher Education,* 1980, *23* (15), 271–282.

Tinto, V. "Dropout from Higher Education: A Theoretical Synthesis of Recent Research." *Review of Educational Research,* 1975, *45,* 89–125.

White, C., Pascarella, E., and Pflaum, S. "Effects of Training in Sentence Construction on the Comprehension of Learning-Disabled Children." *Journal of Educational Psychology,* 1981, *73,* 697–704.

Phillip Beal is dean of students at Saginaw Valley State College, University Center, Michigan. He was formerly a visiting scholar at the National Center for Higher Education Management Systems where he codirected the What Works In Student Retention *study.*

Ernest T. Pascarella is professor of evaluation research, College of Education, University of Illinois–Chicago.

Some generalizations are made about important issues in the study of student attrition.

Concluding Thoughts

Ernest T. Pascarella

As attested to by the preceding chapters, persistence/withdrawal behavior in postsecondary institutions is the result of an extremely complex set of influences that are not yet completely understood. At the same time, however, an underlying theme of this sourcebook is that theoretical and methodological tools exist to enable institutional researchers to study the phenomenon systematically. While not intended to be prescriptive in any sense, this sourcebook has tried to present issues for institutional researchers' consideration in the study of attrition. These issues can be summarized as follows:

1. Defining student attrition is not always a simple, straightforward task. Depending on one's perspective, leaving an institution (or postsecondary education generally) can have many different meanings. As Tinto has suggested (Chapter One, this volume), not all dropping out is bad, nor should it be of concern to institutional researchers. In operationally defining attrition, then, it behooves us to give considerable thought to what withdrawing means to the student, as well as to the institution. In terms of influencing policy, the most useful studies will probably focus on withdrawal that has harmful consequences for student development and which the institution can take positive action to prevent.

2. Until recently, most attrition research was descriptive and atheoretical, resulting in a large number of individual investigations that were difficult to synthesize into a meaningful body of knowledge on which to base policy. The different theoretical models discussed by Bean (Chapter Two, this volume) are potentially powerful blueprints to guide institutional researchers in

E. Pascarella (Ed.). *New Directions for Institutional Research: Studying Student Attrition*, no. 36. San Francisco: Jossey-Bass, December 1982.

the various aspects of attrition study (for example, variable selection and assessment, parsimonious research design, and data analysis). If future research is to contribute to a generalizable, systematic body of knowledge aimed at understanding the underlying processes of attrition, it is important that single-institution studies be guided by theory.

3. From a methodological standpoint, the most valid results will very likely come from attrition studies that, in addition to being guided by theory, are (a) longitudinal in design, following the same cohort of students over a specified period of time; (b) take into account differences among student background characteristics by measuring such aspirations, aptitudes, and competencies prior to enrollment on campus; (c) collect in-depth, multiple measures of the extent and quality of students' interactions with different aspects of the institutional environment; and (d) employ multivariate analytical procedures that permit us to assess the unique influences of various aspects of the college experience, while controlling for the influences of differences in aspirations, aptitudes, and competencies that students bring to college.

Of these concerns, perhaps the most important are those of data quality. Since what happens after a student arrives on campus may be at least as important to persistence/withdrawal behavior as preenrollment characteristics, it is important for institutional researchers to give considerable though to reliable and valid assessments of students' experiences of college. In terms of policy, such assessments may be most valid if they focus on aspects of students' experience that institutional decision makers can influence purposefully.

As is often the case, the type of study yielding the potentially most valid results may be the most difficult to conduct in terms of human and financial resources. Against this problem, however, must be weighed the cost benefits and value of the data provided.

4. It may be possible to develop programmatic interventions at the institutional level that positively influence student persistence. To date, however, the evaluation of these interventions has seldom gone beyond the level of preexperimental or nonsystematic verification. Because such interventions are potentially significant contributions to policy as well as to knowledge, they clearly deserve more rigorous experimental and quasiexperimental verification of their effects. It is important that such verifications also give attention to specific underlying dimensions of the intervention that lead to the results observed.

5. Finally, student persistence/withdrawal behavior is influenced by a variety of institutional practices and aspects of the institutional environment. Thus the study of student attrition forces institutional researchers to confront some very fundamental educational activities at their institution (for example, admissions policies, academic quality, teaching quality, intellectual development, student–faculty interaction, and the quality of residential life). Thus, one of the less obvious but potentially important benefits of institutionally sponsored research on student persistence/withdrawal behavior is that research

may lead institutions to look critically at the very processes by which they educate students—and it is after all, the education of students that is a fundamental reason for institutions' existence.

Ernest T. Pascarella is professor of evaluation research at the University of Illinois–Chicago. For the past seven years, he has conducted numerous studies of student persistence/withdrawal behavior and its impact on colleges. He has a special interest in how faculty members can socialize students informally.

Additional sources of information are presented
for researchers in student attrition behavior.

Resources for Research on Student Attrition

David W. Chapman

The following references are provided to assist researchers concerned with the design and conduct of attrition studies. These references represent only a part of the growing literature in this area; they were selected for their comprehensiveness and/or recency. Many of the entries contain additional bibliography, should a reader wish to extend this list. The references below are organized into eight categories: (1) reviews and syntheses of research on attrition; (2) models offered to explain student attrition; (3) questionnaires and survey instruments previously used and their research history; (4) the names of national educational associations and organizations that provide information, materials, and/or help to researchers in this area; (5) selected multi-institutional studies of student attrition; (6) selected single-institution studies; (7) examples of interventions designed to reduce attrition; and (8) a list of funded projects currently under way.

Reviews of Literature and Syntheses of Previous Research

Astin, A. *Preventing Students from Dropping Out.* San Francisco: Jossey-Bass, 1975.
Astin, A. *Four Critical Years.* San Francisco: Jossey-Bass, 1977.
Borup, J. H. "A Synthesis of Research on College Dropouts and Guidelines for the Future." *Tains,* 1968, *1,* 21–36.

E. Pascarella (Ed.). *New Directions for Institutional Research: Studying Student Attrition,* no. 36.
San Francisco: Jossey-Bass, December 1982.

Cope, R., and Hannah, W. *Revolving College Doors: The Causes and Consequences of Dropping Out, Stopping Out, and Transferring.* New York: Wiley, 1975.

Henderson, C. "Retention Improvement: Selected Case Studies." ACE Policy Brief. Washington, D.C.: Division of Policy Analysis and Research, American Council on Education, 1980.

Jackley, J., and Henderson, C. "Retention: Tactics for the Eighties." ACE Policy Brief. Washington, D.C.: Division of Policy Analysis and Research, American Council on Education, 1979.

Jackley, J. P. "Postsecondary Student Retention Studies: An Annotated Bibliography." Washington, D.C.: Division of Policy Analysis and Research, American Council on Education, 1980.

Lenning, O. T., Munday, L. A., Johnson, O. B., VanderWell, A. R., and Brue, E. J. *Nonintellective Correlates of Grades, Persistence, and Academic Learning in College: The Published Literature Through the Decade of the Sixties.* Monograph 14. Iowa City, Iowa: American College Testing Program, 1974. (ED 105 324)

Lenning, O. T., Sauer, K., and Beal, P. E. *Student Retention Strategies.* AAHE-ERIC/Higher Education Research Report No. 8. Washington, D.C.: American Association for Higher Education, 1980.

Noel, L. "Reducing the Dropout Rate." In L. Noel (Ed.), *New Directions for Student Services: Reducing the Dropout Rate,* no. 3. San Francisco: Jossey-Bass, 1978.

Pantages, T. J., and Creedon, C. F. "Studies of College Student Attrition: 1950–1975. *Review of Educational Research,* 1978, *48* (1), 49–101.

Racioppo, V. C. "A Computer Model to Simulate Institutional Change for Increasing Student Persistence at Small Liberal Arts Colleges." Unpublished doctoral dissertation. Iowa City: University of Iowa, 1981.

Ramist, L. *College Student Attrition and Retention.* College Board Report No. 81-1. New York: College Entrance Examination Board, 1981.

Rootman, I. "Voluntary Withdrawal from a Total Adult Society." *Sociology of Education,* 1972, *45,* 258–270.

Valiga, M. J. "Institutional Variability in the Causes of Attrition." Paper presented at the annual forum of the Association for Institutional Research, Atlanta, Ga., April 1980.

Models to Explain Student Attrition

Bean, J. "Dropouts and Turnover: The Synthesis and Test of a Causal Model of Student Attrition." *Research in Higher Education,* 1980, *12,* 155–187.

Pascarella, E. T. "Student–Faculty Informal Contact and College Outcomes." *Review of Educational Research,* 1980, *50,* 545–595.

Spady, W. G. "Dropouts from Higher Education: Toward an Empirical Model." *Interchange,* 1971, *2,* 38–62.

Tinto, V. "Dropouts from Higher Education: A Theoretical Synthesis of Recent Research." *Review of Educational Research,* 1975, *45,* 89–125.

Questionnaires Used in the Study of Student Attrition
and Their Research History

Institutional Integration Scales. Available from either Dr. Ernest Pascarella, College of Education, University of Illinois at Chicago Circle, Box 4348, Chicago, IL 60680; or from Dr. Patrick Terenzini, Director of Institutional Research, 301 Administration, State University of New York at Albany, Albany, NY 12222.

Research using the *Institutional Integration Scales* includes:

Pascarella, E. T., and Terenzini, P. "Interaction Effects in Spady's and Tinto's Conceptual Models of College Dropout." *Sociology and Education,* 1979, *52,* 197–210.

Pascarella, E. T., and Terenzini, P. "Predicting Freshman Persistence and Voluntary Dropout Decisions from a Theoretical Model." *Journal of Higher Education,* 1980, *51,* 60–75.

Terenzini, P., Lorang, W., and Pascarella, E. T. "Predicting Freshman Persistence and Voluntary Dropout Decisions: A Replication." *Research in Higher Education,* 1981, *15,* 109–128.

Student Involvement Questionnaire. Presented in R. H. Johnson, "The Relationship of Academic and Social Integration to Student Attrition — A Study Across Institutions and Institutional Types." Unpublished doctoral dissertation. Ann Arbor: The University of Michigan, 1980.

Additional research that has used the *Student Involvement Questionnaire* includes:

Chapman, D. W., and Pascarella, E. T. "Predictors of Academic and Social Integration of College Students." Paper presented at the annual meeting of the American Educational Research Association, New York City, March 19–23, 1982.

Johnson, R. H., and Chapman, D. W. "Involvement in Academic and Social Activities and Its Relationship to Student Persistence — A Study Across Institutional Types." Paper presented at the annual forum of the Association for Institutional Research, Atlanta, Ga., April 1980.

Pascarella, E. T., and Chapman, D. W. "A Multi-Institutional Study of a Theoretical Model of College Withdrawal." Paper presented at the annual meeting of the American Educational Research Association, New York City, March 19–23, 1982.

Student Outcomes Questionnaire. Available from the National Center for Higher Education Management Systems (NCHEMS), Boulder, CO 80302. Most studies have been internal, single-institution studies. Contact NCHEMS for more information.

Student Turnover Questionnaire. Available from Dr. John Bean, Department of Higher Education, 236 Education Building, Third and Jordan, Indiana University, Bloomington, IN 47405.

Research that has used the *Student Turnover Questionnaire* includes:

Bean, J. "Dropouts and Turnover: The Synthesis and Test of a Causal Model of Student Attrition." *Research in Higher Education,* 1980, *12,* 155–187.
Bean, J. "The Application of a Model of Turnover in Work Organizations to the Student Attrition Process." *Review of Higher Education,* forthcoming.
Bean, J. "Student Attrition, Intentions, and Confidence: Interaction Effects in a Path Model." *Research in Higher Education,* forthcoming.
Bean, J., and Cressell, J. W. "Student Attrition Among Women at a Liberal Arts College." *Journal of College Student Personnel,* 1980, *21* (4), 320–327.

Withdrawing/Nonreturning Student Survey. Available from the ACT Evaluation/ Survey Service, The American College Testing Program, Institutional Services Area, P.O. Box 168, Iowa City, IA 52243. Most studies have been internal, single-institution studies. Contact ACT for more information.

Selected Educational Associations and Organizations Involved with Research on Attrition

American College Testing Program, P.O. Box 168, Iowa City, Iowa 52243.

Beal, P. E., and Noel, L. *What Works in Student Retention.* Iowa City, Iowa, and Boulder, Colo.: American College Testing Program and the National Center for Higher Education Management Systems, 1980. (ED 180 348)
Noel, L., and Renter, L. *College-Student Retention — An Annotated Bibliography of Recent Dissertations, 1970–March 1975.* Iowa City, Iowa: American College Testing Program, 1975.

American Council on Education, One Dupont Circle, Washington, D.C. 20036. The ACE Division of Policy Analysis and Research primarily serves as a clearinghouse for research conducted by other agencies and institutions. For such assistance, contact Ms. Cathy Henderson, Research Associate, Division of Policy Analysis and Research, American Council on Education, One Dupont Circle, Washington, D.C. 20036. See also:

Astin, A. *College Dropouts: A National Profile.* Vol. 7. Washington, D.C.: American Council on Education, 1972.

Henderson, C. "Retention Improvement: Selected Case Studies." ACE Policy Brief. Washington, D.C.: Division of Policy Analysis and Research, American Council on Education, 1980.

Jackley, J. P. "Postsecondary Student Retention Studies: An Annotated Bibliography." Washington, D.C.: Division of Policy Analysis and Research, American Council on Education, 1980.

Jackley, J., and Henderson, C. "Retention: Tactics for the Eighties." ACE Policy Brief. Washington, D.C.: Division of Policy Analysis and Research, American Council on Education, 1979.

Educational Testing Service, Princeton, NJ 08541.

Ramist, L. "College Student Attrition and Retention." College Board Report No. 80-1. New York: College Entrance Examination Board, 1981.

Patrick, C., Meyers, E., and Van Dusen, W. *A Manual for Conducting Student Attrition Studies.* Boulder, Colo., and New York, N.Y.: National Center for Higher Education Management Systems and the College Entrance Examination Board, 1979.

National Center for Higher Education Management Systems, Boulder, CO 80302.

Beal, P. E., and Noel, L. *What Works in Student Retention.* Iowa City, Iowa, and Boulder, Colo.: American College Testing Program and Higher Education Management Systems, 1980. (ED 180 348)

Bower, C., and Myers, E. *A Manual for Conducting Student Attrition Studies in Institutions of Postsecondary Education.* Technical Report No. 74. Boulder, Colo.: National Center for Higher Education Management Systems, 1976.

Lenning, O. T., Beal, P. E., and Sauer, K. *Retention and Attrition: Evidence for Action and Research.* Boulder, Colo.: National Center for Higher Education Management Systems, 1978. (ED 156 098)

Patrick, C., Myers, E., and VanDusen, W. *A Manual for Conducting Student Attrition Studies.* Boulder, Colo., and New York, N.Y.: National Center for Higher Education Management Systems and the College Entrance Examination Board, 1979.

Multi-Institutional Analyses of Student Attrition

Research using data from the National Longitudinal Study of the Class of 1972:

Anderson, K. "Post-High School Experiences and College Attrition." *Sociology of Education,* 1981, *54,* 1–5.

Munro, B. H. "Dropouts from Higher Education: Path Analysis of a National Sample." *American Educational Research Journal,* 1981, *18* (2), 133–141.

Peng, S. S., and Fetters, W. B. "Variables Involved in Withdrawal During the First Two Years of College: Preliminary Findings from the National Longitudinal Study of the High School Class of 1972." *American Educational Research Journal,* 1978, *15* (3), 361–372.

Other multi-institutional research on attrition includes:

Johnson, R. H. "The Relationship of Academic and Social Integration to Student Attrition — A Case Study Across Institutions and Institutional Types." Unpublished doctoral dissertation. Ann Arbor: The University of Michigan, 1980.
Pascarella, E. T., and Chapman, D. W. "A Multi-Institutional Validation of a Theoretical Model of College Withdrawal." Paper presented at the annual meeting of the American Educational Research Association, New York City, March 19–23, 1982.

Selected Single-Institution Studies

Only published studies are included:

Aitken, N. "College Student Performance Satisfaction and Retention: Specification and Estimation of a Structural Model." *Journal of Higher Education,* 1982, *53,* 32–50.
Baumgart, N., and Johnstone, J. "Attrition at an Australian University: A Case Study." *Journal of Higher Education,* 1977, *48,* 553–570.
Bean, J., and Cressell, J. "Student Attrition Among Women at a Liberal Arts College." *Journal of College Student Personnel,* 1980, *21,* 320–327.
Churchill, W., and Iwai, S. "College Attrition, Student Use of Campus Facilities, and a Consideration of Self-Reported Personal Problems." *Research in Higher Education,* 1981, *14,* 353–365.
Durio, H., and Kildow, H. "The Nonretention of Capable Women Engineering Students." *Research in Higher Education,* 1980, *13,* 61–71.
Pascarella, E. T., and Terenzini, P. "Patterns of Student–Faculty Informal Interaction Beyond the Classroom and Voluntary Freshman Attrition." *Journal of Higher Education,* 1977, *48,* 540–552.
Pascarella, E., Duby, P., Miller, V., and Rasher, S. "Pre-Enrollment Variables and Academic Performance as Predictors of Freshman-Year Persistence, Early Withdrawal, and Stopout Behavior in an Urban, Nonresidential University." *Research in Higher Education,* 1981, *15,* 329–349.
Terenzini, P., and Pascarella, E. T. "Voluntary Freshman Attrition and Patterns of Social and Academic Integration in a University: A Test of a Conceptual Model." *Research in Higher Education,* 1977, *6,* 25–44.
Terenzini, P., and Pascarella, E. T. "The Relation of Students' Precollege Characteristics and Freshman-Year Experience to Voluntary Attrition." *Research in Higher Education,* 1978, *9,* 347–366.

Selected Published Reports on Interventions Designed to Reduce Attrition

Pascarella, E. T., and Terenzini, P. "Residence Arrangement, Student–Faculty Relationships, and Freshman-Year Educational Outcomes." *Journal of College Student Personnel,* 1981, *22,* 147–156.

Pedrini, B., and Pedrini, D. "Evaluating Experimental and Control Programs for Attrition/Persistence." *Journal of Educational Research,* 1978, *71,* 234–237.

Rossman, J. "An Experimental Study of Faculty Advising." *Personnel and Guidance Journal,* 1967, *46,* 160–164.

Rossman, J. "Released Time for Faculty Advising: The Impact Upon Freshmen." *Personnel and Guidance Journal,* 1968, *47,* 385–393.

Selected Funded Projects Currently Under Way

The Tennessee Higher Education Commission has received a two-year grant from the Ford Foundation to study the determinants and consequences of educational progress for minority students. The study, which is based on samples from over twenty-five universities in six states, will also consider persistence as a dependent measure. For more information, contact Dr. Michael Nettles, Project Director, Tennessee Higher Education Commission, 501 Union Building, Suite 300, Nashville, TN 37219.

Dr. Paul Dressel, with a grant from the Exxon Educational Foundation, is studying the impact of academic program characteristics on student persistence in college. As part of his project, titled "Persistence: A Second Look," he has contacted over 700 colleges for information on rates of student persistence across academic programs and how students' changes of academic program influence their rates of persistence. For more information, contact Dr. Paul L. Dressel, Professor of University Research, A310 East Fee Hall, Michigan State University, East Lansing, MI 48824.

The NCHEMS-Kellogg Student Outcomes Project, directed by Dr. Peter T. Ewell, addresses two growing concerns in higher education: the outcomes of higher education and using information effectively. The project ties together activities under way at seven participating institutions. While this project is not primarily focused on retention, several of the institutions are using student outcomes to access or influence attrition. For more information, contact Dr. Peter T. Ewell, National Center for Higher Education Management Systems, P.O. Drawer P, Boulder, CO 80302.

The Higher Education Research Institute (HERI) is currently conducting several projects related to student retention. The Southern California Retention Consortium, a project funded by the Kellogg Foundation, involves several private, liberal arts colleges working together to increase retention and improve student outcomes. The institute also conducts an annual freshman survey as part of the Cooperative Institutional Research and Assessment Project. As an extension of that activity, HERI conducts institutional follow-up studies, which include students who leave the institution prior to graduation. For information on either activity, contact Dr. J. Victor Baldridge, Higher Education Research Institute, University of California, Los Angeles, CA 90024.

David W. Chapman is assistant professor of education,
State University of New York at Albany.
He was previously director of evaluation for Project CHOICE
at the University of Michigan.

Index

STATEMENT OF OWNERSHIP, MANAGEMENT, AND CIRCULATION
(Required by 39 U.S.C. 3685)

1. Title of Publication: New Directions for Institutional Research. A. Publication number: USPS 098-830. 2. Date of filing: September 30, 1982. 3. Frequency of issue: quarterly. A. Number of issues published annually: four. B. Annual subscription price: $35 institutions; $21 individuals. 4. Location of known office of publication: 433 California Street, San Francisco (San Francisco County), California 94104. 5. Location of the headquarters or general business offices of the publishers: 433 California Street, San Francisco (San Francisco County), California 94104. 6. Names and addresses of publisher, editor, and managing editor: publisher — Jossey-Bass Inc., Publishers, 433 California Street, San Francisco, California 94104; editor — Marvin Peterson, Center for Study of Higher Education, University of Michigan, Ann Arbor, MI 48109; managing editor — Allen Jossey-Bass, 433 California Street, San Francisco, California 94104. 7. Owner: Jossey-Bass Inc., Publishers, 433 California Street, San Francisco, California 94104. 8. Known bondholders, mortgages, and other security holders owning or holding 1 percent or more of total amount of bonds, mortgages, or other securities: same as No. 7. 10. Extent and nature of circulation: (Note: first number indicates the average number of copies of each issue during the preceding twelve months; the second number indicates the actual number of copies published nearest to filing date.) A. Total number of copies printed (net press run): 2058, 1873. B. Paid circulation, 1) Sales through dealers and carriers, street vendors, and counter sales: 85, 40. 2) Mail subscriptions: 925, 884. C. Total paid circulation: 1010, 924. D. Free distribution by mail, carrier, or other means (samples, complimentary, and other free copies): 125, 125. E. Total distribution (sum of C and D): 1135, 1049. F. Copies not distributed, 1) Office use, left over, unaccounted, spoiled after printing: 923, 824. 2) Returns from news agents: 0, 0. G. Total (sum of E, F1, and 2 — should equal net press run shown in A): 2058, 1873.

I certify that the statements made by me above are correct and complete.

JOHN R. WARD
Vice-President